TransVerse II

No Time for Silence

Words of Survival, Resilience and Hope

Edited by Dr Ash Brockwell

First published 2021 by Reconnecting Rainbows Press

www.reconnectingrainbows.co.uk

ISBN 978-1-8383-4251-7

To that person who needed to read this today

(you know who you are):

You are enough.

You are valid.

You are loved.

Introduction

Since the first 'TransVerse' anthology was published in August 2019, the COVID-19 pandemic has changed the world beyond all recognition. Trans and non-binary people who were already struggling with dysphoria, transphobia, rejection, loneliness and all the other issues covered in the original anthology now have even more problems to deal with. Long-awaited surgeries are being postponed indefinitely, waiting lists for gender clinic appointments are getting longer, injections are being cancelled, and the availability of hormones, blockers and other essential medications – even through private providers – can no longer be taken for granted.

It doesn't end with access to health care. Thousands of vulnerable trans people around the world are being isolated from their friends, counsellors and peer support groups, and forced to live with relatives who misgender and deadname them on a daily basis. On top of all that, there's the generic trauma of living through a pandemic, which affects cis and trans people alike – anxiety about getting the virus and spreading it to others, fear of losing loved ones, breakdown of comforting routines, loss of social spaces and face-to-face mental health support, extreme stress from something as simple as a trip to the supermarket, all manner of PTSD-related responses to all manner of triggers, and vast oceans of grief for the small losses as well as the big ones. Many of these issues are making life especially difficult for neurodiverse people, who tend to be strongly represented in the gender-diverse community.

Black trans women and other transfeminine people of colour face even greater challenges - the 'toxic trio' of racism, misogyny and transphobia. In too many cases, they're accompanied by police brutality (or, at best, indifference) and laws that criminalise the expression of LGBTQI+ identities with long prison sentences – sometimes life imprisonment – or even the death sentence. You'll find stories and poems from the Refugee Trans Initiative in Kenya, along with Black trans people in the UK and USA, throughout this book.

But trans and non-binary people are incredibly strong and resilient. We wouldn't be here if we weren't! Everything we've already endured has helped us to build our coping skills, including the ability to find small glimmers of hope in the midst of the trauma – or even if we can't see them, to trust that they exist somewhere, like stars on a cloudy night

The idea for this book was born in response to an all-day interactive digital festival celebrating the diversity and creativity of the trans and non-binary community, organised by a UK charity Mermaids to support, uplift and inspire young people struggling with social isolation. A young trans poet touched people's hearts with a poem on the theme of 'Surviving', and many of the other guests spoke to a similar theme, along these lines:

This period of our history is tough, but we will get through it. We have the skills, the strength and the strategies – and, most importantly, we have our solidarity.

When I put out a call in the online trans community for poems about surviving, I was overwhelmed by the response. We didn't get mere survival: we got hope, resilience, love, happiness, joy, gender euphoria, trust, freedom, pride, courage, rebellion, humour, assertiveness, revolution, beauty, inspiration, defiance, faith, determination, and a celebration of trans and non-binary identities of all different kinds.

While TransVerse 1 had 26 contributors, this time we've doubled that number. This book unites writers from four continents, and just like the original volume, it includes first-time poets on an equal footing with professional singer/songwriters. There's no judgement of contributions on the basis of their supposed `literary merit': quite apart from the fact that we've all faced more than enough judgement from people around us, who are any of us to judge another person's unique voice and self-expression? Who are we to say that a word doesn't fit here, that a rhyme scheme feels awkward there, or that a poem shouldn't be included because it pushes our buttons? We're all valid, we're all enough, we all write from the heart, and we can all be that 'voice in the wilderness' for someone who's struggling.

On that note, a word about triggers: if the original TransVerse anthology was like a menu, grouping poems and lyrics together by theme with specific trigger warnings for each section, this book is more like a huge, delicious buffet. I haven't even tried to subdivide or classify the contributions, as so many of them touch on multiple themes, and I wanted them all to speak for themselves. Another difference is that this time around, I've invited contributors to share a bit more about their lives if they want to. These longer stories are included alongside the poems. (Everyone still has a 100-word bio at the end of the book too).

Please be aware that you might come across something triggering, especially in the life stories – I've included trigger warnings at the start of some individual contributions, but that might not always be enough to prevent a problematic word from catching your eye. If that happens, please stay safe, turn the page, and you'll hopefully find something to lighten the mood – and if you're still struggling with difficult memories or disturbing thoughts, please reach out and ask for support. Helpline numbers are at the back of the book.

Wherever you are in the world, may these poems, stories and lyrics remind you that you're never alone. May our words inspire the will to survive, the power to build resilience, the courage to hope, and the determination to thrive. Please stay safe, stay strong, and stay proud of who you are and who you're becoming.

We're going to be OK.
We're going to be more than just OK.
We're going to *thrive.*

And on that note, I'll hand over to Barbie Midna Pyka for our first poem. Editors shouldn't have favourites, but as someone who's just beginning to shift out of `surviving' mode and into `thriving' mode, this particular poem resonated with me on a whole other level. Hope you enjoy it – and all the other wonderful contributions, too.

Dr Ash Brockwell PhD FRSA (he/him)
March 2021

Contents

Thrive
Barbie Midna Pyka

Once upon a time,
I would've been okay just surviving.
Once upon a time, that's all I wanted,
I would say,
"I just want to survive, is that too much to ask?"

I don't just want anything anymore,
I want to thrive
I don't just want to live
I want to thrive.
I want to succeed.
I want people to look at me and say,
"That! That right there is one hell of a comeback story."

I want to thrive.
I don't just want to make ends meet,
I want to make banks beg for my business.
I want producers to come to me and ask to fund my stories.
I want to be able to say,
No, I want to quote The Pacifier
"There is no highway option."

I want them to be falling over themselves-
No, each other and groveling
Saying, "Yes, of course. Nonbinary lead? Of course! Let's go!"
"Aromantic story? Sure!
I don't know what aromantic means, but let's do it!"
"A diverse cast and crew? That's actually diverse?
Sure! I'm down!"

I want them begging on their knees, saying,
"Yes, yes. Whatever you write.
Just let me put my name on your success."
"Just let me ride your coattails."

I don't just want to live,
I'm done with barely surviving.
I want to thrive.
I want to succeed.
I want to make a name for myself,
But most of all?

I want kids like me to look at that big, silver screen,
And say,
Look. That's me.
They got a happy ending. I can too.

I want them to look at me and say,
They did it. They made it.
Maybe I can too.

Maybe I'm done barely surviving.
Maybe I want to thrive.

That's what I want them to say.
That's what I want to hear.
I'll know I'm thriving when
I can order something on the menu without looking at the price.
When I can just pick up and go on vacation out of nowhere.

And I'll know that I'm successful, truly successful,
When I hear the kids in my stories say,
I deserve a happy ending.

I deserve to thrive.
I deserve to be successful.

I'll know when I hear,
I am done barely surviving.
I am done with just wanting to live.
I am done asking to survive.
I will thrive.

I will tell you all this, right now.
If surviving is asking for too much,
Then I'm done asking.

And no amount of haters, no amount of dark thoughts,
No amount of negativity will stop me.

And do you know why?
Because writing? Is my vent.
And if you thought the shit I've already been through was fuel…

I'm a queer, polyamorous, asexual, greyromantic, bi-something,
genderfluid enby
Who uses they/them, he/him and *gem* pronouns.
Do you have any idea how many people that is going to piss off?

And more importantly,
Do you know how many people I am to inspire?

I am going to thrive.
I am going to succeed.

Dear trans person
Frogb0i

Dear trans person,
You are not too much.
You are not a burden.
You are not unworthy of love and respect.
You do not need "pass" or "look cis".
You are not defined by other people's perceptions
or interpretations of you.
You don't need to compare yourself to others,
Because no one else is you.
No one else has gone through what you have...
Because no one else is you.

You have survived your darkest days...
...And you are here still.

You are important,
Loved,
Individual
And one of a kind.

You matter,
You have bloomed,
I see you,
And you deserve the world.

Dear Trans Person,
Remember.
Existing itself is a form of rebellion.

Dear cisgender person

Autumn Barkley

When you're trying to imagine what it's like to be transgender, don't try to imagine what it would be like to be a gender you aren't, because that isn't what we feel, and it's too difficult to conceptualise for most people anyway.

Imagine being a fruit. Bear with me.

You are an apple.

You grow up in a world where on the basis of features you had no choice over, people call you a pineapple.

This feels wrong, you aren't a pineapple, but adults do seem to know a lot, so maybe they're right?

Over time, mostly without thinking about it too hard (after all, there's Lego over there and this gender stuff really is too upsetting to think about when you could be having fun!), you come to think you are a pineapple. You live as a pineapple, you're treated as a pineapple, it might not even occur to you to object to it because it's been told to you for so long, and you certainly don't tell anybody you think they're wrong.

At this point, you have internalised a lie about yourself, because you are a child, and in general regardless of age it is quite difficult to resist such sustained mental pressure over a long enough period of time.

Adolescence comes, the bodies of yourself and your classmates diverge, you become depressed but you can't really figure out why. Sure, you joke with your friends, there are moments of happiness, but there's this....thing, hanging over you. Whatever you do it won't seem to go away.

You look at the apples in your class and unlike the other pineapples you aren't focusing on dating them as much as you are jealous. They get to be what you can't ever be. You've been told so many times you can be. What you've always sorta known you were, or at least wanted to be - after all, you're a pineapple, you can't be anything else. Everyone else knows better. You know better.

The distress gets worse; being reminded of what you are hurts. You avoid mirrors, you try to ignore your thoughts. You feel like you must be mad.

Then comes the reading, the discovery, talking about it with others. You aren't alone. You're pretty sure you're an apple and you've found community of people who have also been gaslit into believing this lie you've been told, and even told yourself, for so long. You begin to dig yourself out of this pit of self delusion and become more frustrated with a world that you know is wrong. You tell your parents, they reject you, scream, cry....

Imagine what it's like to be told a lie, internalise that lie, figure out it is a lie, find other people who also know, tell other people what is clearly the obvious truth that all these people seem to have figured out - even scientists have looked into it, there are entire world associations for scientists looking into it, and then be rejected for it. Retold the lie.

More than that, realise that because seemingly so many people believe this collective lie, you not only have less rights than before but you're at higher risk of homelessness, disease, assault, medical malpractice, and murder, because some people really take comfort, even joy, in enforcing this lie. Most people just go along with it. Thoughtlessly.

That is what being transgender is. At least for me. It's fighting a collective delusion, and sometimes self-delusion, that I'm not what I've really always been, even if only in a way I couldn't put to words at first.

Small things become very important over a long enough period of time, so it's vital you don't let them pile up in the first place. Thoughtless comments like "you can't do that, you're a boy".

It turns out having your voice ruined by puberty really forces the issue mentally though. I used to sing all the time, and yes, most of what I sang was written by other women. Now I can't remember the last time I did. Mostly I try not to think about it. When I try to explain I don't usually have the words.

That's what being transgender is.

No more lies. Please.

Rebuilding trust
Dalton Harrison

Rebuilding trust,
That turned to dust,
More smoke in my eyes,
Then lies.
I'm telling jokes to hide my worsted fears.
Yet these tears feed my demons.
Who sit in my chest banging ribs tearing at heart strings.
I'm looking in the cracks and seeing broken,
but you fill it with gold and tell me I'm the token,
The thing you've been missing
and I don't believe in miracles!
 Not since my mum died while I was still inside,
but there you stand with outreached hands.
You look at me like I'm the thunder bolt from Zeus hand.
Like I'm the strength you needed,
yet I was never anyone's hero,
 just a villain, the Joker.
The moral to the story,
but you hold me and you tell me,
I am your ocean
and I think of all the times I was told I was worthless,
a mess of floating debris
yet you said I was your sunken treasure!
You held me in the storms I created,
In all the chaos!
You looked at me like I was the map to your lost,
the key to your door!
No matter how I mourned
the me before sin coated me in paint,
you looked at me and said I was a rainbow!
 I know now what it feels like to finally breathe
with you as my Queen,
 I will rebuild the trust that left me.

Woman, Warrior, Queen
Queen Victoria Ortega

Men come up to me
they say hello and asks for my name
before I respond I remember the pain.
Memories of rejection and laughter.
I ask myself
do I answer
do I have a choice?
and I hope
he doesn't notice
 my deep voice

I answer "Queen Victoria"
and then they walk away saying "shit!"
 Angry at having been "fooled"
But fret I do not
for a shield and dagger I have tooled
They can't tell me what to do
How to look or how to sound
For by the binary – I am not bound.
I refuse to fake my voice and sound
like someone stuck a helium tube up my ass.
I am me
and that's that.

Do I sound different?
Do I look different?
Ya dam Skippy!
And I love myself for it.
That is my real strength
and our real strength of my community.

We know that all the odds
are against us at this point in history,
my culture devalues trans women because we said –
fuck male privilege –
in order to live as our authentic selves.

We don't have job opportunities
nor access to trans affirm healthcare
we are not looked at as viable life partners

and shit
if we get real
I mean really real
 not even our gay lesbian and allies
know what to do with us

but why do we persist you ask?

– because we are so dam powerful
so so dam real, dam beautiful,
and so dam resilient
that we must show the rest of humanity
what the fuck it means
to personify the word
chingona
or
badass

see that is my story and my heritage
 I am Queen Victoria Elizabeth Marie Josephine Ortega
the Woman Warrior,
and the fucken Queen.

Car Boot Questioning
Eden Irving

Is this right?
Am I lost?
Is this where the sale is?
What is all this?

> *One set of Pride pins.*
> *All labels used.*
> *Give to someone they will fit.*

How do you pronounce half of these?
How much for this?
Do I know who I am?
Who do I want to be?
Why do I hate this now?

> *One blue suit.*
> *Worn once.*
> *Never again.*

Why is THIS here?
Why did I do that?
How couldn't I see before?
Was it that obvious?

> *Three books on gender.*
> *40x post-its inside.*
> *They come free.*

Do I need this though?
What 'scent' is my gender?
What does that even mean??
How far do I go?
How far will they let me get?
How big is too big?

> *One 5ft Pride flag.*
> *Bought two*
> *in ecstatic rush to have one.*

Where's my wallet!?
What do I say?
What should I do?
Should I even come out?
What would I tell them?
Is the truth what they want from me?

> *Three books on Christianity.*
> *Give to someone who'll*
> *find answers better than I.*

Where's the exit?
Which way out?
What if they doubt me?
Where to start?
How does tucking work?
How much do I want to change?

> *One pair of shoes.*
> *Newly applied rainbow laces.*
> *Take care of them.*

Do I even know what I'm saying?
Are the mirrors lying to me?
Am I enby?
Am I enby enough?
Does that even matter?

> *Four months with a family*
> *that won't understand.*
> *No refunds.*

Should I go?
Who do I turn to?
Will they hate me?
Will they believe me?
Am I depressed?
…Am I?

> *Three years of Questioning.*
> *To be concluded.*

What's this label?
What's that label?
What ARE these labels?
Do I need a label?
Can I borrow your label maker?

> *One Amazon delivery.*
> *Sent to wrong address.*
> *Do NOT open on arrival.*

Why is my body so shit?
Why doesn't it feel right?
Am I lucky?
Am I selfish?
What is it about looking andro?

> *Four packs of makeup.*
> *Lost in house move.*
> *Apply with care.*

Why does 'boy' feel wrong?
He or she?
How do you know?
What IS my hair?
Why do I like it this way?

> *One hundred and one*
> *gay fictional characters.*
> *All new. All found. Yet to be written.*

Will I ever find love?
Will I ever be loved?
How do love yourself?
Is any of this worth it?
What's with all the questions?
Why am I here?

> *One lost person.*
> *Second-hand, past sell-by date.*
> *Will find themselves soon.*

Oh.
Yeah.

Returns
Jon/Joan Knight

I remember as if yesterday
The time you first told a joke
You told it me twice in quick time.
Even if I had not listened,
I could see the laughter in your eyes.
Who could be deaf to that?

And, with your pre-emptive almost laugh,
You hooked up from my depths
A huge chunk of joy
That I had previously dropped.

You handed it back to me
On a simple joke.

Later, that night
I cried a little with happiness
And then duly laughed.
At the joke yes,
yet also
With incandescent hope.

(This is from my time as a school form tutor, I had a student that had had the shittiest of childhoods – he had been basically rescued by foster parents but was deeply scarred emotionally. He was in my tutor group for four years and it took three years for him to speak openly with the others. In the final year he flourished into who he could be. Every day was not always forward, but week on week I was lucky to see one of the most amazing and beautiful occurrences: the rebirth of a human spirit.)

Love Letter to LGBT+ Youth

Bingo Allison

I believe in you
Not like some half-assed Disney princess would say
Spout the shit then clear the popcorn away
Not some sunset backed emotional insta
Some inane balls scrawled on a coaster
I'm talking real belief
In the currents that run beneath
In what used to be called heart and soul
In all those splintered parts glued together to make a whole
In the realness

I believe in you
I believe in the colours of the rainbow on your wrist
In the power of your mind and your fist
In the risks you take
In the lives you make
I believe in you

I believe in you
When you're walking down the street holding hands
When they're shaking drinking tea at your nan's

In the family you'll find
In the ones you leave behind
I believe in you
 I believe in you
In the sheer fucking cleverness of you
In the way things go that you set your mind to
In the places you'll go
In the horizons you'll know
I believe in you

So take this as a sign
Trust these thoughts and words are mine
Whatever trouble, whatever time
Whatever joy fills your lungs
Trips out over your tongue
Whatever crap fills your head
Whatever shit your mother said
Whatever else I do
I will keep on believing in you
Because people like you set me free
People like you made me want to believe in me

French Braid I and II
Kei Patrick

I

I see a French braid,

(I think)

the kind I never learned to make

as a boy

threads

shining

in one way or another,

folded over and under

(maybe around)

into a rope

.

I remember 8-year-old hands

sat on the carpet,

working together at the back of someone's head,

someone who had long hair,

though it was never me,

though I did.

We would be sat on the carpet

listening (I did)

receiving a lesson,
and the workers would be gently admonished

for not paying attention.

.

"Listen."

They all knew the secret:
>how to turn their face to the front,
>and with their hands
>keep working on the braid.

They knew
that if they faced the teacher, they would be allowed to continue
>with the necessary work of weaving braids together.

All of them were little girls.
When I look back at that scene,
>(I see a teacher tutting with a smile,)
I see it from the outside.
I see the backs of their heads.

II

I see a French braid

(I think)

on the back of my head.
The shoulders of my back are slightly uneven,

it gives me character.

Across the shoulders of my back is the worn, maroon silk
      of my Dad's old shirt, which I took with me from home.

My hair is longer now than it ever has been:
if this braid were on the back of my childhood head
as I sat on the carpet in Year 3,

(I must have done,)

it would coil on the floor.

I'm going on stage today, buoyed up by my friends,

who painted my eyes,
who glittered my cheeks,
who did
the necessary work
of making the braid,
they did: three of them offered,
one of them wove it;

by my Dad, who gave me his old shirt,
in which I have grown to wear glitter and a braid
that reaches my shoulder blades.

And looking back at this scene, I see the back of my head.

Fight for Equality
Red Fraggle / Beck Alsford

My dream was to help the homeless
not be one of them
knew I wanted to change the world
since I was 10

but working class people
can't get upper class jobs
16 years at uni
but I'm still treated like a yob

You shouldn't of come to uni
if you couldn't afford it
your help for the disabled
doesn't amount to shit

You wanted to defeat me
You wanted me to give up
"we've never dealt with this before"
ie: fuck off and shut up

But I didn't do either
my soul won't be defeated
out of my destiny
I refuse to be cheated

So prepare for the freight train
of my solid conviction
I will fight for equality
until my extinction

Eva

Te Urukeiha Tuhua

you're just confused
i feel so sorry for you
are you sure you even know God
my best friend said
and so i tried to
shrug off her words but they stuck
like a wad of glue
inside i felt myself wilt
was i doing this for
attention
was i just
a fake

many months later i came out
of my closet
trembling and shaking
i screamed
i am non-binary
people looked at me with pity
you're a girl
they called me by my dead name
refused to accept
me
i faded slowly away
feelings bottled inside
locked away

a few weeks later i
met another enby
they uplifted me
told me it would be okay
took me under their wing
with their guidance i joined
social groups
people who gave me validation
and i think
i think
it will be okay

.

.

Non-Non-Binary
Bingo Allison

The non in the nonbinary has nothing now to do with me
it's...not
And the knots which my poor stomach makes as the knowing no
my heart it shakes...a lot
I will not be forgot
The naming of my names as none
with empty bags of nada nuns...they're gone
The hiding of the hidden side there's no one to enjoy the ride...
there's none

And I've got no time for nothing
When this fullness makes me smile
When the quintessential queerness
Comes and sits with me a while
And so you'll find me genderqueering
With the nellies and the butch
So much more than nothing
With the longing and the touch
And when the blessed binary
Is finally gone
I'll still be queering happily
Engendered beyond none

I'm Back (lyrics)
Elliott Boot

I've tried this one too many times
I think I've finally got this right, this time
I've never connected with my mind
And what I've found has come as no surprise
And now...

I'm back
Didn't I tell ye
I'm back
Better than ever
I'm back
So, you've gotta
Watch your back 'cause
I'm back
Didn't I tell ye
I'm back
Better than ever
I'm back
So, you've gotta
Watch your back 'cause
I'm back

In case you missed this miss became a mister
And now my brother's got a brother not a sister
And ain't nobody crying that, that they miss her
'Cause this here mister is ten times happier than
She would've ever bin, that's why I'm celebrating
By scratching out the lyrics like the master Ed Sheeran
 Leaving room to drop the beat like my vocal cords
For my new husky voice darlin' praise the lord

It's been a long time coming and there's still time to come
And more to be done and songs to be sung
But in the meantime, I guess
I've gotta let everybody know that…

I'm back
Didn't I tell ye
I'm back
Better than ever
I'm back
So, you've gotta
Watch your back 'cause
I'm back
Didn't I tell ye
I'm back
Better than ever
I'm back
So, you've gotta
Watch your back 'cause
I'm back

I may seem weak but I'm actually just nice
I'm so tough I went through puberty twice
And our lot in life's just a roll of the dice
But any roll can be both good and bad in different eyes
Like for me being born in the wrong body sucks
But having a supportive network was nothing short of luck
'Cause there's people out there that'll tell me
that a pig can't be a duck
But I'm not the one rolling around in the muck
Dragging other people
down with me…

It's a mystery,
why we can't let people be happy
the way that they wanna be,
I'm finally seeing clearly,
I'm finally where I'm meant to be
And no one on this planet
can take that away from me

'Cause I'm back, with my new name and my old face
I'm back, with a new style but my old taste
I'm back, no need to elaborate or hesitate
Now come on over here and join me as I celebrate

This transition is what I gotta do
I'm evolving into something old and new
This transition's got nothing to do with you
I'm evolving into something whole and true

This transition is what I gotta do
I'm evolving into something old and new
This transition's got nothing to do with you
('Cause I'm back, didn't I tell ye, I'm back better than ever,
I'm back, so you've gotta watch your back 'Cause…)
I'm evolving into something whole and true
(…I'm back, didn't I tell ye, I'm back better than ever,
I'm back, so you've gotta watch your back 'Cause…)

I'm back.

My Life – Elliott Boot, UK (he/him)

I've never been the most confident person. I always felt I had something holding me back. A haze of self-doubt I was constantly immersed in that I could never find my way out of. At least not completely.

When I was 18, I left home for university. Hoping to lift some of the mist before I succumbed to it. That worked for a while. I was "one of the guys". But nothing lasts forever. The fog was starting to creep back in. I wanted to cling onto what I had so I chose to do a postgraduate degree.

So, there I was in a new university, new people. Then that year was also over. That's when the panic set in. I wasn't happy with who I was and I didn't know why or what to do next with my life.

The fog around me had started to creep back, thicker than before. I couldn't see. I was trapped.

Then a hand came through the mist and took mine. My best friend. The same friend from the first day of my undergraduate degree. Who I worked and lived with. She sat down next to me when I was at my worst and said, "Do you think you're transgender?".

Someone had spoken out loud something I had been subconsciously avoiding for years. Then the dominoes just kept falling. I went on to Google as you do with all the big questions in life and I bought the book "You and Your Gender Identity A Guide to Discovery" by Dara Hoffman-Fox, LPC.

I had finally found the answer to so many questions in my life. Finally had the determination to explore that part of myself. And finally, the fog had started to disperse.

Two years later to the present. I'm 25 years old. I'm 14 months on testosterone. I'm training in mixed martial arts, something I have always wanted to do but never truly believed I was capable of, and close to achieving my black belt.

I'm writing again. I'm looking towards hopefully being a wedding performer one day, or a singer/songwriter, as now I believe I am good enough.

I'm finally happy when I think of what I'm doing with my life. I'm happy to live with my parents for now while I save money. I'm happy to be single as I know I need to work on myself so when the right person comes along, I'll be ready. I'm happy working in a job that might not be what I want to do forever, because they have been fantastic with my transition and I get to work with my best friend who I honestly believe saved me.

All these things just two years ago terrified me. But I now have a brand-new perspective on life. I've survived the worst and the future can only be brighter. I'm now the most confident version of myself so far. And every day is like a clear blue sky with the perfect view.

I Was Silent
Kestral Gaian

[Trigger warning: attempted suicide]

People ask me why
I talk so much.
Like maybe I don't know that it's rude,
Or every silence need not
be filled.

I tell them, they too would talk for England,
if only they knew.
Knew what it was like,
to not be able to talk at all.

I was silent,
for so long -
not a poem or verse,
not a sound or a song,
or anything, really,
except what I thought
that I was expected to say,
The things I ought,
to say or do or think
or feel or know or hate or love.

I was silent,
for so long -
I still spoke, I still screamed,
every sound from my throat stinging like acid,
My words leaving my tongue red raw,
my gums bloody, teeth worn.

Not an honest thought -
gaslighting myself -
or the imposter with my face-
telling me that I should stay silent,
and let them talk in my place.

I was silent,
for so long -
a girl with a muzzle made
out of peer pressure and social anxiety.
A woman on a leash, wrapped in chains,
so deeply buried that even Narnia's
most observant fauns couldn't find
the back of the closet
I had locked myself within.

Silence. Not of voice. But of spirit.

And I was silent,
for so long -
I blew out candles, 18, 19,
wishing for my freedom,
20, 21, why won't my wish get answered?
22, 23, 24 - no more.

The me that the world sees has taken over,
Where is my voice?
Why does the end not just come?

I try - too weak to take enough of the tablets,
Too silent to explain why, as my boyfriend sobs,
wondering if it's because
of him.

He always thinks it's because
of him.

I stopped being silent on a Tuesday afternoon.
A day as plain and insignificant as my life had become -
the words like milk,
soothing the wounds in my mouth that had been open,
for so long.

I am a woman. I am here.
I am me.

I was silent,
for so long -
And I'm still learning.
Still finding my voice,
still outing the imposter.
Still wishing on a candle.
Still learning. Always learning.

But I was silent,
for so long -
too long.

No more.

Identity
Dalton Harrison

What is identity inside these walls,
Doors so thick it binds the chest you hide so you can't breathe,
Define me by numbers,
 a sign that says female estate,
I can't deny I'm here,
 but I'm just visiting,
Yet still I see the dirt tracks of ghosts walking in rows,
 the smell of death like somehow
that was the only way to ever be free,
What is identity,
 identify me in societies hallow walls,
where no one hears you cry in towels,
 given used and repeated in a system
that deals with mass incarceration,
 this blue towel in my hand that I leave the streaks in,
 my sobs, my grief, my guilt, my past,
I could wring it out tear it in half in anger,
But I sit with this feeling that stretches across from hand to hand
I look and wonder in the middle of my pain
in the pinnacle of my fallen tears,
if anyone used this as a noose to stop theirs,
I throw it aside and it coils around like a viper in the room,
 I feel the poison, I taste it on my lips,
 I feel it in my body,
what is identity,
the system is they/them,
I am the boy behind the wall and the sign says female estate.

Lazaret
Jani E Z Franck

You're a cocoon waiting emptily
For me.

Sunlight plays across your floors
Day by day, unseen.

Everything from the moments before
Captured, a capsule of former life.

In corners, spiders weave
The quiet story of this waiting.

In the raw emptiness outside
I transform, skin bared to the rain and wind. You
Are silent, living your own story
Somewhere else, across the waters.

These empty rooms,
Filled with plans and
Deep desire.

The windows rattle in the wind,
Curtains hanging silently,
As the seasons pass outside.

The moon watches us, she
Has seen this many times, she
Knows where the story will end.

I am constant motion, the trees
Flail above me, blossoms
Fallen now, leaves growing to fullness.

Later,
I shall gather shells into my sodden shirt,
I shall tread barefoot down the path
Stones and thorns beneath me
Thunderclouds above me,

Following the faint glimmer of a candle
In our window.

Each step leading me home to
The never-forgotten, constant
Dream
Of you before of me.

(A lazaret is a quarantine station for seafarers)

Cimex lectularius
RKP

.

.

I'mma poet like heart surgery,

Get your scalpels,

Wanna piece of me?

Cannibalize those thoughts with knives,

Cos everyone wants some

Aorta know better,

But there's no anaesthetic,

Grab gurneys'n'watch for the drip.

Judgements are sharp - ain't wise -

No shepherds for guides.

Plunge the morphine,

I can see halos falling,

Controlled substances course veins,

Lemme open the can of worms,

Truth serum,

Pull apart for it's abstraction,

Like rotten crowns grinning along jawlines,

This broken smile of the century for a septic tank of a story,

The eldest MacPhearson,

Went and got a dog collar,

Leashed to God'n'mortar,

Amethyst streetlights down Hull roads,

With some pups'n'a Parish to call his own.

Hiding behind religion,

N'yeah I know the postcode -

Keepin' evil eyes close to the diocese.

While ya work on that poker face when you preach,

To sheep in pews grazing on holy communion bread'n'wine.

Do you ever get nostalgia,
Eagerly prizing a young girls fingers...
Under blankets - awake.
Smothering innocence to an early grave,
Signing the stone..."it was me".

Remember your gaze into the congregation
when you exchanged vows.
I remember the squeeze of Kathy's hand to stay silent...
N''Forever hold your peace."
Is the room still enough for prayer,
Like dissociating paralysis?
Flashbacks - frozen body underneath,
With a slow building flame.
Matthew, Mark, Luke and John,
Do they Bless the bed you lay on,
Four corners to the rug I've been swept under,
Do ya wonder...thinkin'?
Nah no one will believe the crazy,
Ranting' and ravin',
Or have you begged forgiveness,
Something mediocre,
Gettin' away with murder,
Fearing Revelations,
The Alpha..Omega..
Judgement of the Lamb.
Service to the cloth for righteous places at The Almighty's side.
Prodigal daughter truths,
From Parkside cell block rooftops,

Your born again Mother heard the camel backs snap.
She burst into a cry something biblical,
Busting for heathens,
Cursing my existence.

N'if I'm going to hell,
Then there's a room with a view,
Priced high for the sins of a heart,
Weigh it against a feather...
The scales will fall ringing out a redemption sound,
For a freedom found in the dissection of historical happenings.
Words that'll bury at the second,
6feet high,
Count it'n'go down.

Now that the bough

Alex Francis

Now that the bough has shed her blossom
Now that the sky is lighter turned
Up to the air I fix my senses,
Up in the scarlet clouds they yearn:

To see your face, a ruddy fire,
Rubescent swathes of fragile air,
Stripe greedy seas of glowing embers,
Alight my love, abandon care.

With petal soft, once pure white darkened,
And fallen from its host of bark,
Lay sullen next the sodden roots,
'mongst grass so green,
we'll view the stars.

Now shining 'tween a world of darkness
Each glittered jewel spells out our love,
Down to the earth we'll wander slowly
Down from our crimson world above.

Now that the bough has shed his bounty
Now that the sky is curtain closed
Up in the air I lose my senses:
Still as the clouds, our love reposed.

No
Quenby Harley

Aha no it doesn't stand for ally, it actually means asexu-. No, actually trans people have existed fo-. No bi isn't the same as gree-. No, that's not-. Um no actual-. No. No. No. NO.

I am done modulating my voice
Explaining every choice
I've made in the life I've lived
And I am done speaking for the privileged

I'm tired of being the punchline
Of people thinking it's fine
To make a joke about being trans or gay
And laugh at people who hear this every fucking day

I'm tired of people who talk about free speech
When that's the only human right they preach
The people who are fine reinforcing a prejudice
Which says I don't have the right to exist

Queer identity isn't a topic for debate
Pretending otherwise exposes a world of hate
A cascade of intolerance and disgust
Directed towards us

Because behind "protecting the kids"
There's an ideology that forbids
People who aren't cis and straight
Being spared from vehement hate

And when it feels like the world hates you
You know what you do?
You internalise that shit
You start to believe it

And it's not just words, I can't escape this
When I walk down the street I risk facing a fist
I choose between endless stares
And dysphoric despair

Calls for civility are a call for silence
A call to look away from a history of violence
Civility allowed people to ignore our plague
Using euphemisms and language vague

Cos homophobia
Is a phobia
An irrational fear
Of people who are queer

And if you're scared by me then so be it
Because whether or not you believe it
I'm scared too
I'm scared of you

I'm scared of becoming another sad statistic
And that's not just me being pessimistic
Our past and our existence is often a mystery
Because of silenced voices and erased history

So I will fight
For the right
For my voice to be heard
To not be treated as anomalous or absurd

I speak now to my queer sisters and brothers
Who've spent their lives being treated as others
Now is our chance for change
To not be seen as inhuman or strange

Today I say no to all this bullshit
Together, we can fight it
So be proud
Be fucking loud

Celebrating

Eris the Vogon

It's insane, an entire year
Completely free of fear
Not homeless, out on my ear
Celebrating trans survival
In my own life's happy revival

Onward and upward
Moving ever forward
To a body restructured
Celebrating trans hopes
In my body's changing envelope

Looking to tomorrow
Shall I climb Kilimanjaro
With joy, without sorrow
Celebrating trans resilience
In my mind's rich experience

I Am They, I Am Or.
Barbie Midna Pyka

"He or She?"
"Him or Her?"
"You must be one or the other."
"You must choose."

That's what is said.
But that's not true.

Oh, no.
It's decided for you.

Often before birth.
but I am neither.

I am they.

"He or She?"
Or.

"Wrong. Him or Her?"
Or.

"Not an option."
They.

"Not an option."

I don't care.
I am they.
I am or.

"She."

It is decided for me.
I ignore that decision.

"Then she-"
They. I correct

Blank stares.
Dirty looks

"She."
They.

Don't ask him or her.

Stupid questions get stupid answers. I decide.
My life, my name, my pronouns.

I will not allow *them* to be ignored.

I am not "he".

I am not "she".

I am or. I am they.

Survival Advice Given to LGBT Refugees in Kenya

Doreen Andrewz

A gay couple cannot walk together holding hands,
because they are at risk of dying.

A trans woman cannot wear high heels,
or lipstick,
because that could be her death.

A trans man has to be forced to put on a dress or a skirt,
all in the name of keeping a low profile
and staying safe,
because you will die if you don't do that.

You will die if you try to be yourself.
If you try to love who you're supposed to love,
if you try to expose your true self,
who you really are,
that could be the death of you.

You can't walk the way you walk usually.
Find a new way to walk.
You can't talk the way you talk as usual.
Find a new voice.

Trans woman: if you're too feminine, it's going to lead you to death.
Find some masculinity in you!
Trans man: be more feminine or you will die!

That's the advice.
That's the advice that they are giving us
On how to stay alive.

My Life – Doreen Andrewz, Kenya (she/her)

[Trigger warning: transmisogyny, anti-trans violence]

I'm a trans woman who hasn't fully gone through her transition yet., because in Africa it's not easy to access therapies – no access to hormones, no access to surgeries – but I will. I have to. I have to fully live my life.

I'm currently a refugee in Kenya. I've been in Nairobi for years because of security issues as a trans woman. I had attended Kakuma, a place where refugees from wars are living and they're not expecting to be resettled somewhere else. This is their home, this is their future, this is where they're going to live the rest of their life, and this is where UNHCR [United Nations High Commission on Refugees] is putting LGBT refugees even up to now. They don't have anywhere else to put them, so we can't blame them! But the situation is wrong, the system is not right.

LGBT refugees cannot be put in this place because it's outing who we are already; the camp is not so big, and everyone knows everyone. As an LGBT person you are illegal in Kenya; the Kenyan law does not support LGBT people at all. They don't have any legal representation. Actually, the law is set to arrest anyone who is found out to be gay, for 14 years! So the police itself does not feel the obligation to give us any of their services.

I'm talking about transgender people who are left in a neighbourhood that is homophobic because of tradition, because of religion, because of cultural beliefs, because men believe 'a man should be a man and a woman should be a woman'. The neighbourhood that the LGBT people are living in is violent, it's angry, it's not allowing people to live their lives. They know the police are not going to come in and intervene when some LGBT person gets beaten or cut or slapped. Do not be surprised if you hear one day that one or two LGBT refugees died in that camp called Kakuma. Do not be surprised!

But I'm a trans rights activist and a human rights defender. Some other trans people call me I'm the Assistant Executive of Refugee Trans Initiative and I'm also going to mobilise in Kakuma. I try to stand for the rights of transgender people – to stand against injustice that we go through, to see how best we can fit into the community and see how we can live our lives, right through the trauma and struggles of our identity, and how best we can be productive in society.

I Didn't Audition
Red Fraggle / Beck Alsford

I didn't audition
for this cis gender show
but god gave me a front bottom
39 years ago

I'm hoping the curtains
will go down pretty quick
because wearing these pronouns
is making me really sick

will your baby be blue
or will it be pink
why need you sexualise it
 before it can think?

And just so you know it
before the world wars
both genders wore dresses
until age of 4

Lost and found
Kay Whitehurst

I had a house, I had a wife,
I had some money, I had a life,
I had a car with lots of class,
I had expensive tools to cut the grass.
I had weekends in the sun,
I had film nights, lots of fun,
I had everything a guy could want
I had the dream life some had hoped for.

But still I wasn't happy, and still I wasn't sane,
There was something burning in my brain,
The thoughts that had been there since youth,
The crushing and ever destructive truth.
That this was all a lie, and I,
was acting, playing, this part to die,
A demon sat there curled within,
Faking all that I was him.

I cried alone in the window seat,
I cried alone in the shower,
I pretended I was sickly sweet,
Whenever she gave a glower.
Yet I cried and cried and cried again,
Almost many times slit a vein,
For I knew what was held inside,
Yet I couldn't let go of this stubborn pride

See I had done such a perfect job,
convincing everyone, trying to fob
them off with falsehood and play my part,
That I'd convinced myself it was my true heart,

Yet every week a moment came,
Where I could suddenly remember the pain,
Buried it deep and covered it again,
Hold my head up and walk in the rain.

The truth is that I had those times,
The me I was was always me.
Gender was only the outward means
Of showing the world what they wanted to see.
The me that was then exists even now,
Though not convinced by your shallow vow,
And when you said that I had changed
All you could see were the outside chains,
Being unshackled, released, reversed.
You should have been happy, instead you cursed
me and left me for dead in the pool of despair,
I loved you but you never loved me.. So there..

I had the house, the car, the wife,
I even had that 'perfect' life,
But all was given and all was lost,
When I paid the ultimate cost,
Of being me, we could have been much more
Yet you trampled our "love" on the floor,
And therein you played what was in your heart,
Not truly loving just playing the part.
You wanted someone to be your Joseph,
No matter who or what they chose, if
You wanted them to be something they would,
And the reward was your conditional love.

I had the car, the house, the wife...
But truly, honestly, it wasn't my life.

The Real Trans Happiness
Kei Patrick

We begin with dead space,
        blind spots,
        holes in second-hand clothes
        badly loved.

The real trans happiness must be glamorous somewhere in black silk
        must be glittering in comfy clothes with an easy laugh.
    This is just a pile of denim.

We clear the way by taking up this waste material
        and cutting off the sleeves first, teasing out
        tangled knots of thread, cutting some off altogether.

We sew on patches,
        carefully unpick old names from
        the neckline or embroider them into

                a burst of new
                flowers growing
                under the collar.

Fuck dress sizes. This is
        a collage,
        tapestry,
        a stencil cut to fit my dreams, silhouette
        my shoulders.

The real trans happiness is handmade with forgiven fabric and old card,
    a craft knife on the kitchen table working new patterns into old wood.

Nothingness

Kyle Warwick

An empty sky, full of thoughts,
A breath of fresh air, full of regret,
A blank piece of paper, fill with terrifying images,
Isn't it amazing,
How nothing can seem like everything?

Everything provides an illusion,
In a girl's body there may be a boy,
And in a boy's body it may be a girl.
Nothing may be everything
While everything may be nothing.

Staring into nothingness
Can provide a window of thoughts,
Staring into thingness
Could be the difference between life and death.

In my life,
Nothingness is my saviour.

The system
Dalton Harrison

[Trigger warning: prison]

I am shackled,
Made to feel less then human,
The shadows mimic movements,
But they are mocking me,
I am currently formless,
I am suddenly voiceless,
my face, like me, is forgotten,
No image reflects back in smudged scratched plastic,
Hate fuelled enabling environments
Justice served in a system of care leavers, beaten women, addicts,
sex workers abused fill criminology students case files,
Designed to build a suitable system to house us,
Use words like depraved, vile, evil,
That and leave us to wet ourselves in transport wagons that secure us
For public safety,
For the public's best interest is to make me feel inhuman,
 To make me stifle my cries of fear of using up too much oxygen,
To lock me in one-way-seen rooms to leave out air
because that's for the free!
To treat me like cattle to the slaughter,
 Numbered tagged and delivered is my favourite bedtime story,
 I am one!
Of a percentage that managed to live,
Line my mind with charts,
Pretty colours don't reflect much!

In the system is only dead babies and blood stains,
screaming echoes and buzz words,
Years of alarms and code blues code reds,
Twisted up to the seg,
No room for real issues,
just wait till you get out!
Ex-offenders are where the story starts.

nobody listens to kids like me
Te Urukeiha Tuhua

nobody listens to kids like me
i am never taken
seriously
because when i'm nervous i
overuse slang words like
chur
so when i say i'm nonbinary
i'm ignored
and i get scared easily
and i'm scared of telling
my classmates and teachers
about my pronouns

i'm scared of getting
frequent migraines
i had one last week
and i don't want to
face my fears because i
have so many fears
i'm scared to turn off my light
i don't want to be trapped
in the dark

i want people to hear me
but nobody does
i cry a lot into my knees
wishing
for the things i don't have

i know i will get through it i have
gotten through a lot
in this life
once i was left outside
in the cold for hours
when i was a baby
i survived that

Confused
Barbie Midna Pyka

"You're just confused."

Excuse me?
Confused?
Me?

Have you met me?
I am almost always confused about something.

Like. Biology.
Punnett squares? Genetics?
Gimme a quick review packet and I can do it.
The rest of Biology? I ain't got a clue.
I'm very confused about biology.

Or…
It is difficult for me to say Pythagorean Theorem,
I can hardly say it, but the actual formula?
A squared plus b squared equals c squared, very easy.
I love math.
But not geometry.
Fuck geometry, actually.
And screw trigonometry.
SOHCAHTOA can sohcahsuckmyass.

I'm confused about-
Oh?
What's that?

Oh!

Oh, you meant my gender.

Whoops.

I'm definitely confused about gender.
What's the point of it?
I don't get how you can just have one?
Why do you get to dictate mine?
Why do genitals equal gender?
The only thing they have in common is the letter G.
Okay! And the letters N and E.

I'm confused about gender alright,
But I know I'm genderfluid
I know I'm genderpunk.
I may not always know what my gender of the day is,
But it sure as hell ain't tied to my bottom text.

Bodies
Frogb0i

Their scars were in the same place as mine,
And as our bodies intertwined,
My mind realised that for the first time in my life,
 I felt pride to be body alive.

Genitals are not the main course.
Frogb0i

I am yet to find a cis gay man who makes me feel divine.

They cannot spare the time to learn, that my trans body has differen
buttons and switches that must be carefully aligned; and that their ci
genitals are not better than mine.

Their satisfaction is not more important than mine.

They don't earn a gold star of "ally ship" for interacting with my body

Their genitals are not the main course. It should go as follows:

Starter:

Words - whispered,

Hands - held,

Neck - kisses, Hair - twirled

Main course: Me

Main course: Me

Main course: Me

Dessert: cis gay man

Finally Me
Keelin McCoy

I always felt trapped
Like I was stuck in a hole
And although it was hard to start
I could vision my end goal

I hated the sight of myself
My reflection caused me tears
But there was a lot to look forward to
If I overcame my biggest fears

I now know it's not wrong
And certainly not a sin
To want to look on the outside
The same as I felt within

I reached out to fellow peers
And I realised I wasn't alone
Through these wonderful friends
My confidence has finally grown

It's been a long road
But I'm now free from pain
I could never have had the rainbow
Without experiencing the rain

I'm thankful for the support
The light I could finally see
My journey was totally worth it
At last, I am finally me

Coronavirus
Mickie Leigh

[Trigger warning: illness, bereavement]

In the middle of a bleak day,
Shops closed, buses slowed,
Cars no longer swarm the road.

Victims of death increase by hour,
Hospitals fill, Conservatives still in power
Front-line workers fall ill.
Trump wants to bring out, disinfectant pill.
No protective gear for doctor or nurse,
As this virus drives its way
Like some evil curse.

Front liners face violence just doing their work,
As others are trapped in, unable to go out.
Living in a new kind of normal,
Is feeding the nation's doubt.
As people wonder if things will remain this way,
Should they allow their children to go out and play?
Should we wear masks or cover our face?
The dangers are there for the whole human race.

People lose jobs they clung to,
Once dear.
As loved ones are told,
We are not allowed near.
Yet relatives in nursing homes,
Confused, don't understand,
They simply long to hold our hand.

A pint of beer shared in a pub with friends,
Seems a long way off if this virus ever ends.

And nobody knows if a vaccine will be made,
But we are told to not be afraid.
Yet people grow closer
As they share the same goal
People ask, "what is the current death poll?"
It's all over the news,
As a newborn baby dies,
As relatives grieve,
We hear parent's cries.
None of us know,
If life will return to the way it was before.
Or if Coronavirus will win its bloody war.

There was a time when Corona was just a pint of beer,
But now it's instilled some new kind of fear.
The summer is coming,
We can smell it in the air,
Yet we sit in our homes wishing we were elsewhere.

Our hair is growing longer,
Items in shops sell out,
"Stay well, keep safe" people shout.
Soap addicts wonder how long it will be,
Till Coronation Street is not on TV.
Concerts are cancelled,
Pride doesn't take place.

It tries in its power to beat and kick us down,
Yet we will grow stronger,
We will swim, not drown.
We put up a fight
Supporting the NHS
We've lost so many people
Coronavirus might try to pull us apart,
But, it doesn't know the strength of the human heart.

My Life – Mickie Leigh, UK

[Trigger warning: sexual abuse, spiritual abuse, dysphoria]

My name is Mickie and I'm non-binary. I have two genders, male and female. Sometimes it feels as though I'm in-between genders.

I only realised I was transgender a few years ago. It's not been easy trying to discover my identity in life. Feeling like a man trapped in a female body was confusing. Looking in the mirror, seeing a man, but not wanting to acknowledge it for fear of shame or judgement. I battled with the thoughts of what my parents might say.

I was eight years old when these feelings began; They grew stronger, the older I became. Angry with my existence, I strove to hide the male part of me inside. I'd experience feminine qualities for months and then masculinity. Experiencing sexual abuse as a child by my best friend's brother, I found men disgusting. Accepting part of me as a man was hard.

I started going to Church in my late twenties. The Church taught it was wrong to be gay and demonic to be transgender. They tried to deliver me from being transgender. It appeared to work at first; I suppressed a side of me and pushed it further inside than ever. I got married to a man, like the Church demanded, and although we were the best of friends, our marriage ended 13 years later. We are still friends to this day and he is father to our two beautiful children.

I started going to a Church called "Liberty" inclusive to the LGBT community, that saved my life. I learned it was ok to be a lesbian and non-binary. People even called me by my male name, Mickie, although the Church members were quite surprised when I came out as non-binary because until that point I'd been very feminine. I wore pink clothes and dyed my hair pink, a way of dealing with my inner emotions.

My Church leader organized a meeting where I discussed my experiences of being transgender and from then on everyone accepted me. My Church friends made me realise there was nothing sinful in being true to myself.

Soon after accepting the male part of me, the anger disappeared. Liberty helped me so much. If it wasn't for the Church, I don't think I'd be here today. Until that stage I believed God judged me for being transgender. I ended up realising God loves me and accepts me for who I am.

Spectrum (lyrics)
The Bleeding Obvious

I'm a witchy switchy soft femme queerdo.
A lowbrow aesthete, rainbow heart.
Study your celestials under a night sky.
Glue us together when we fall apart.
Live our ideologies, liberation rituals
Unravel my complexities, I'll revel in yours.
Remind me of the pleasures in your gentle little touches
Sketch your profiles while lost in thought.

We're on a spectrum.
Eccentric perfection.
Ambidextrous momentum.
Live life, love on the spectrum.

Bipolar Gemini, let me have my way
I've a sense of direction with a playful kink
Curl up kitty tell me it's OK
Say what haunts you over a drink
Overly affectionate, needy when I want to be
Kiss me through words, bond with desire.
I'm a human can of silly string, intractable and brilliant
Mix me drinks, see what transpires.

We're on a spectrum.
Eccentric perfection.
Ambidextrous momentum.
Live life, love on the spectrum.

Let's have rabble-rousing rough sex
Transparently androgynous
Fearlessly tender

Taurus as hell.
Fearless tommistry
With Sundays sedentary
Lascivious flirtation
With a genderqueer femme.
We're on the spectrum.

A workboot stud of simple needs
In a new world order, dressed in tweed.
Give me nasty hookups somewhere down south,
You'll love the sound of your name in my mouth.
Strong-jawed sweetie, I'm a 6-foot Aphrodite!
Bond over art, make out in the yard
Or hang around in bookshops while we talk about our analysts
Bruise me with your avant-garde.

We're on a spectrum.
Eccentric perfection.
Ambidextrous momentum.
Live life, love on the spectrum.

Lyrics from the album 'Rainbow Heart', reproduced with the permission of
the artist: https://bleedingobvious.uk/rainbowheart/lyrics

Ten Foot Wall (lyrics)
Elliott Boot

The path ahead
Is somehow blocked
and there seems to be
no way around it
you can't turn back
you can't give up
you're so close
you must keep going now
you must keep going

'Cause standing before you is a ten foot wall
with no view of the other side
but the only thing that's holding you back is yourself
as each brick is formed from the doubts in your mind so
take a run up and knock it down
find its weak point and bring it to the ground
find your strength that's there to be found
'Cause my friend, it's you against the wall.

Brush off the dirt
wipe of the sweat
grit your teeth
stand up and focus
scrape back the hair
out of your eyes
ground yourself
you can do this now
you can do this

'Cause standing before you is a ten foot wall
with no view of the other side
but the only thing that's holding you back is yourself
as each brick is formed from the doubts in your mind so
take a run up and knock it down
find its weak point and bring it to the ground
find your strength that's there to be found
'Cause my friend, it's you against the wall.
It's you against the wall, it's you against the wall

I believe in you
I know it's not easy to do
I've been through this before
So, I know you can conquer your wall

'Cause standing before you is a ten foot wall
with no view of the other side
but the only thing that's holding you back is yourself
as each brick is formed from the doubts in your mind so
take a run up and knock it down
find its weak point and bring it to the ground
find your strength that's there to be found
'Cause my friend, it's you against the wall.
It's you against the wall, it's you against the wall
It's you against the wall, it's you against the wall
It's you against the wall.

Trans Happiness is Real

Kei Patrick

2019, from graffiti stencilled in blue and pink.

The real trans happiness is stencilled
    in blue and pink paint
    onto city bins
    in the early morning.
It comes exploding out of a can.

Carefully we prepare it in the crafting-spaces of our homes.
We cut our stencils from scrap material, carve out our own names and
a space to breathe.
We breathe clandestine colours shimmering into grimy reality.

And after knocking about
    at high pressure
    in a rattling box
    mass-produced in thin tin
    mechanically to collect our distorted voices,
    grinding up against
        some core inside
        the walls
        and our formless colours,
                we begin to coalesce.

Frontbum

Red Fraggle / Beck Alsford

[Trigger warning: dysphoria, genitals]

I've called it a frontbum,
I've called it a foo,
I've called it a cunt,
But there's one thing I can't do.
The medical word for it
Keeps freaking me out,
For me it's part of
What being Trans is about.
My fear of my genitals
Has affected my life,
But I need to face up to it,
I can't deal with the strife.
It's called a VAGINA,
It's part of my body,
It doesn't make me female,
It just means I'm me.

Unaligned Feminine
Bingo Allison

Dragging hair out my tits
Face that sank a thousand ships
Squeezing curves into my hips
Shaving rash on my pits

And I feel it in my blood
The eternal sisterhood
And I get the monthly pains
Flowing through my veins

As the moon to which we pray
Washes a non-existent womb away
And I'm wishing she would stay
But I am not she I am they

So many struggles are the same
We all burn in the same flame
And I would proudly wear the name
And I know it's not the shame
That keeps me from the she
I honour every her but I must also honour me

Unaligned but we're allies
Shout my love up to the skies
Solidarity with my sisters
In all the pain and the blisters
That never rain but they pour
Standing for the same cause

As we hold our personhood
And our bodies they are good
Beaten, broken, misunderstood
United in flesh and blood

How am I? (Lockdown, Day 4)
Ash Brockwell

How am I? Am I OK?
I don't know what that means any more.
I know that I've cried more tears in the past six days
than in the six weeks that went before. But I can breathe,
and I'm grateful for that. I'm working, or keeping up some pretence
of trying. Nothing makes sense; but it makes no less
sense to me than anyone else, I guess. I'm breaking down,
or breaking open, I don't know. But, at least, not dying.

Peeling my life back to the bare bones. Going within,
and going without. Trying to work out if there's
some deeper purpose behind it all, some bigger Reason Why.
Bypassing. Keeping my vibe high. Then not bypassing, because
bypassing doesn't cut it. Diving head-first into the vile mess.
Disintegrating? Healing?
Making friends with the distress I'm feeling?
No idea. Revealing layers of grief that I didn't know were there.
Trying to care. Trying not to care. Who cares? Who knows?
No different, in that respect,
from anyone else, I suppose.

But I'm safe, as far as I can tell.
So I guess I should probably say
I'm doing well.

How about you?

The Transit of Venus

Sydney Cardew

As a child, in starched and stuffy uniform
I observed the transit of Venus
Projected on a sheet of paper
A black spot in the blinding light
Passing just for a moment
And then gone out
Into immemorial space

Will I come again?
When the cold atoms of the still cosmos
Reshuffle themselves in the eternal recurrence
And new stars burn in new skies?
Will my soul, a congery of spheres
Flutter through the waiting rooms of reincarnation
Waving yellow forms at the complaints desk
"And what was the meaning of *that*?"
And will the clockwork boddhisatva
Smile in the way that such things smile
and ask me what I learned from the experience?

Or is this it?

But Venus yet endures in her lonely orbit
I saw her yesterday morning from the hill
Gleaming over the bone white chalk
Shining Luciferian in her acid shroud

Let the brilliant starships come!
The clouds scoured away,
The livid coronae healed
Let the verdant jungles be plucked
From the brains of the dead dreamers
Isis, Ishtar, Inanna
Amtor, Eryx, Perelandra

Let Venus bloom again

Looking for Female
(Extracts from a Craigslist Job Board)

Mattie Mamode

[Trigger warning: genitals]

@@@@@@@lick me@@@@@@
My Queen of Spade
genuine, fun, easygoing
Wanted Sunday (or Monday).
a very mischievous view on life, ideally suit yng
Compensation: Negotiable

(Twickenham)

No experience is needed - just willingness and enthusiasm
Please ask for… no pay
Looking for Female
rule out CD or TV

(Battersea)

looking for an attractive, slim average Caucasian
Looking for old ugly fat mature
looking for something new

(London London)

/Nice bum?
Please be able to accommodate
You need to be hot and happy
You must be comfortable
You are well
Compensation: To Be Confirmed

(Croydon)

I am one of a few gents left
I love a female in shorts
I want to see your pussy in its natural state
I pay to eat :)

(Harrow)

If you are looking for fun get in contact
if my wife is here you need to be discrete
If yng more one fifty money

(Walthamstow)

/Open Minded Mums (Lingerie or Nude)

Wanted. Female. Pleasure/fun
Reward available

(Anywhere)

Girl Looking Forward
Paula Adrianne

I see the young girl playing,
It makes me want to cry,
My childhood could have been like hers,
If I had not complied

I acted like a boy,
Because I felt I must,
Told "that's the way to be,"
By those I'd learned to trust.

I suppressed my femininity,
I tried to be a boy,
But not being true to me,
Was life devoid of joy

I even joined the army,
To show that I was tough,
But became too much to bear
This girl had had enough.

But now I'm looking forward,
I don't mourn my past,
Embracing my inner girl,
I'm gonna have a blast!

TDOR Tribute
Paula Adrianne

[Trigger warning: transmisogyny, violence]

Twenty years have gone by
Since Rita Hester died*
Murdered for being herself
For daring not to hide

We gather here together
Tonight at this TDOR
To remember Rita Hester
And the many hundreds more

Together we are stronger
So let us all unite
To stand up against hatred
Let's start to win this fight

So that one day in the future
We will not need TDOR
Because being killed, for being trans
Won't happen anymore.

I love my big trans family
So until that day arrives
Let's help keep each other safe
Let us all survive.

* This poem was written in 2018

Wild Wild (Little Dream) (lyrics)
Kimmy Katarja

I said I do.
What does that mean to you?
Did we pay our dues, like our ancestors told us to?
We jumped this broom and now I'm stuck with you.
Our mystical fantasies lesser value.
Eve and Adam have questions about our views,
but we have answers that we share between us two.

And I'll follow you with empty dreams
and forever things that I never seen.
Expectations of living queens
and would-have-beens.
We've left the chapter happily after
and I hear laughter of what we tried to be.
We stare at everything that we left
in our wild wild little dream.

Could you catch me from my burning mind,
can you respond to my flashing sign?
Are we Superman and Lois Lane
or are we a sinking man of attached to grain?
What does this mean to you?
Can we complete this puzzle, just us two?.
It bothers me that I'm not in your mind,
the muscle I can't get behind.

And I'll follow you with empty dreams
and forever things that I never seen.
Expectations of living queens
and would-have-beens.

We've left the chapter happily after
and I hear laughter of what we tried to be.
We stare at everything that we left
in our wild wild little dream.

I don't know if I can do this.
I don't think I can do this,
You're not the same fantasy I knew once,
Only a picture I drew once.

I don't know if I can do this.
I don't think I can do this,
You're not the same fantasy I knew once,
Only a picture I drew once.

And I'll follow you with empty dreams
and forever things that I never seen.
Expectations of living queens
and would-have-beens.
We've left the chapter happily after
and I hear laughter of what we tried to be.
We stare at everything that we left
in our wild wild little dream.

My Life – Kimmy Katarja, USA (she/her)

I'm Kimmy Kat for short, a Black 23-year-old Creative born in Jamaica and raised in Cleveland Ohio.

I recently came out as trans some time ago, this new revelation is one of the reasons I wanted to stick to music. All my life I've been bounced around. Foster homes, Psych wards and homelessness take up most of my childhood. I guess not a stranger to adapting. You could say it's my strong suit, so it was only a matter of time before the Binary became something I had to shake.

Pre-Quarantine I usually spent my days teaching dance and musical theatre techniques to children; by night I take the stage as a Drag queen, doing splits from insane heights. Podcasting is also how I shake the creative nerve, *Under the Wig* is the Podcast I co-host with my Producer. It's all the scraps, stories I have a hard time writing about but I want people to hear so I put them there.

I hope when you read my lyrics you get just a peek into what it's like in my head. The songs I wrote are songs that come from the glittery depths of my heart. They're all about perspective and change, I see music as a constant movement. It could be a solid but why would you want it to be?

Lone and Unable
Megan Nightingale

Canvassed within folded bedsheet cavities,
bones aching; joints grinding; avolition in play;
exponential.

Cocooned, blankets flailing in an ersatz gale;
mounded pillows; crumpled curtains to subdue
trails of slivering starlight from the skies.

Alarm rings, crackled thoughts sputter and flurry,
indicative of an increasing hurry to commute to work.
The single bed squeaks, sparse springs straining;
spectacles spinning across the spindly wooden floor.

Shadows lift, sunny otherworld obscurities gleam from
a place where a single is a double and one bed becomes many.
Cracked crutches lie, taped; haphazardly placed;
lying against a dusty, singular chest of drawers.

Blank walls canvas blank frames,
desolate; unreachable; olde. Tendons stretch.
The lone day has begun.

Linear perspective

(Creating a convincing illusion of a three-dimensional space on a flat surface)

RKP

Don't you worry about me -
Imma Fence line perching,
Silent observer,
Insomniac sad Black Sheep loner,
Leaving you with eery word worms.

Repeat these squirms like mantras.

There's a vibration of histories in these gums...
Spittin' controversy's abstracted,
Contrary to popular belief wiv choked Heimlich removers for nature
versus nurture,

Who's crazier...
Or saner?

Standing on fault lines as they pass the blame.
But I embody the refusal to never apologise as a victim of your will,
Even bullshit sticks to a glorified equal.

Split families,
My Tribes,
Weighted with whispers from devils'n'angels on shoulders,
Tickin' off the pros'n'cons for pickin' corners...
Did my resilience shock you, as you turned a blind eye?

Please don't be concerned,
My tightened roaches make it smoother.
Put it in your pipe,

Tokes to be a soother...
Making ugly, beautiful again,
Pre-packaged pretty pain.

The truth is a spike -
Lodged in the back of throats,
Isolate the verse'n'buffer leaky stomach linings'n'swallow,
Soakin' up what you couldn't absorb on your autopilot journey to work.
N'I mean no harm if you're offended,
Justha rantin's'n'ravin's of someone feeling...
Corrupted'n'mislead.

Keep on writin' it down cos they like the view I paint,
Bringing it up close'n'personal if ya need to squint.
Dissect to understand the sentence,
Symbiotic cathartic chest breaks alliterate to emphasise.

What it's taken...
What it takes...

Don't pity me wivva "Oh, poor you....."
N'then offer prayer...
I need that like a bullet,
Ha.
Like the Golgotha of shit in ma head...
Put it on hold...
Witha fist full o'pennies for thoughts,
Whilst they predict my distaster...
As I Stare back at the world like its canvas'd by Artists you've never heard of,
Like Rothko, or Richter.

Beautiful Contradictions
Quenby Harley

[Trigger warning: dysphoria, fatphobia, self-harm, genitals]

Sculpted muscular legs
Speckled with cellulite

A powerful voice
Deep enough to hurt me

I wasn't "born in the wrong body"
My body is my body
I have loved it and hated it
I have hurt it and cared for it

Plump, purpled lips
Framed by a beard

Long lashed eyes and exquisite brows
Set in an extra large head

For 20 years I hated my body
Drowning in a putrid cocktail of dysphoria and fatphobia
Hated every stretch mark and flabby fold
Hated my broad shoulders and outsized hands

Thick, muscled arms
Ending in painted nails

The swell of my breasts
Above a barrel belly

I was taught that looking this way was wrong
That to be fat was to sin
That femme with a phallus couldn't be
I can't simply forget that, but I can fight it

Long, delicate curls tumbling to the left
Away from a brutally shaved skull

An elegant black choker
Around an 18" neck

When did my perception shift?
When builders bum was rebranded as luscious ass?
When shameful moobs became tits for other enbies to envy?
A tangled web unravelling
as fat and femme change from attacks to facts

Beaten up old jeans
And an elegantly feminine top

Sturdy boots
Painted with flowers

My body is a mess of beautiful contradictions
Of things to celebrate and things that irritate
I don't know if I'll ever love my body
But I have learned to live with it

Hope
Jay Rose Ana

Years in the future, I hope people will find,
Memories of different people, many different kinds.
They won't be words of hate or greed,
Instead, I hope they will find,
The words that made the world,
Decide to change its mind.

The seed was planted,
The world it turned,
Feeding the roots as they spread through the earth.
It was never easy, but hope stood fast,
And eventually, with love and care,
Its message bloomed, built to last.

When people find this message,
I hope they will understand,
That feeling of hope,
When offering a person,
A kind word,
An open mind,
A helping hand.

Covid 19 Lockdown Blues
Paula Adrianne

It started out in China,
I read it in the news
But now it's in the UK
I've got the Covid 19 lockdown blues

They've closed down all the pubs
I've run out of booze
Completely stone cold sober
I've got the Covid 19 lockdown blues

They've shut down the office
But there's no time to snooze
I'm working from my sofa
I've got the Covid 19 lockdown blues

Folk are panic buying
There's no paper for the loos
I'm wiping with the curtains
I've got the Covid 19 lockdown blues

This old girl is horny
There's no chance of a screw
So now I've sticky fingers
I've got the Covid 19 lockdown blues

I'm not sure that I'll make it
I've not got much to lose
My heart's failing already
I've got the Covid 19 lockdown blues

Standing solid
Kay Whitehurst

The waters flow beneath my feet,
The heart inside my chest it beats
The life that's given so precious and sweet
From the wellspring of the earth

Precious waters flow into my life and fill my mind
The divine magic impart to me and overflow like wine
And wisdom grant this solitary being
In the fullness of time and tide.

The grass grows slowly upwards, its grooves a precious story
Towards the radiant sun and filled with its everlasting glory
Its roots they dig and find the source of agua down below
The tendrils droop into the source of life for ever more

The trees draw up and fill the knotted bark
Their leaves and branches strengthened by its
Life-endowing spark
Whip and blow and canker in the wind
But standing solid in the dark

Nature knows its own fair lines
She breathes her own fair song
And in the fairness of the day
She verily draws us on

Kakuma, 2020
Doreen Andrewz

[Trigger warning: anti-trans violence, police brutality]

we approached them
peacefully

we just sat
at the front of their compound
peacefully

we just sat there

we didn't hold any chants
we weren't holding any rants
we weren't making any riots

we
just
sat
there

even sleeping there

because we were already pushed out
by the community
that is rejecting who we are
we were pushed out of that community
we did not have any place to exist there

and what they did,
they called police

five trucks of police came,
five trucks
filled up with police officers,
carrying boxes and boxes of tear gas
about six boxes of tear gas

they started shooting live fire in the air
live ammunition
and telling us
get out of this place
get out of this compound
go back to wherever
you were living in the camp

we had escaped from our houses
when they were being burnt

imagine, you escaped from people
when you have been raped,
and you leave that place
and go and seek safety from an agency
that is expected to protect you…

and they tell you to go back in that same house
where you have been violated

by force,
with bullets in the air,
caning us with real big canes
and tear gas

we don't have any hope
we don't have any expectation
to even be available
to be alive
to be able to talk
to be able to smile.
we don't have hope
because there is no hope

we are stuck
we are trapped in this camp
and there is nothing we can do about it.

we tried to raise our voice,
we tried,
and they shot bullets in the air
in front of us.
Pointing the guns at us, telling us,
you make one move, we put you down!
you're already an abomination!'

that officer just seeks one excuse
to kill you and he will feel proud,
he will feel like he has done his religion right
by killing a gay person.

we can't do much about this anymore
our hands are tied

but you can.
You can.

Me Myself & I (lyrics)
The Bleeding Obvious

Did you think I'd stumble?
Did you think I'd stall?
Without you there to catch me,
I'd fall?

I'm doing fine thank you
I don't need your safety net
My life is so much simpler
All proportionate.

Freefall - dragging you down
Freefall - up off the ground
Freefall - bounce back stronger.
Freefall - life hits you hard
Freefall - caught off your guard
Freefall - bounce back stronger.

Taking the next plane home
You left me all alone
Don't even call
We don't speak at all

I walk the line each day
It didn't have to be this way
Someday we might meet
Say something bittersweet

Looking back's for fools
I'm breaking all the rules
Keep it in the past
Me myself and I - at last.

Close the door, don't need you any more
Close the door, don't want you any more
Close the door, don't have me any more.

Lyrics from the debut album *The Bleeding Obvious,* reproduced with the permission of the artist. https://bleedingobvious.uk/debut/lyrics

2020 Vision: humanity@where?
Ash Brockwell

In those days when the Ancient Ones left tracks,
They knew the waterholes, the trees, the cracks in every rock.
They left their legends there, embedded in the sand. The land
was theirs, and they were song: the long millennia unable to erase
the histories of their days. The spiral spun. The Stories had begun.

With 20:20 vision, what is seen? Our tracks
are everywhere, the world is all our home,
a toxic foam of ocean laps each ravaged land. We understand
so much, and yet so little. All our songs
are virtual now, our songlines are invisible, the path is far from clear:
@here, and everywhere, we neither know nor care
for ancient ways. Our days drift by. What might we leave behind
for those to come? The sum of our existence:
is it garbage, nothing more?

Coiled inside, our power source, a rainbow serpent still:
in every house unseen, directing trails we cannot comprehend.
How will it end? @chaos, or revival?
Could these wires turn to songlines for survival? Hmm…it seems
we still have dreams, but they are hard to find. The busyness
of business-mind, the cash, the trash, the poisonous addiction
to this fiction ('we can have it all, and here, and now') have
smothered them somehow. Yet even now, if we could tell
those ancient legends once again, we might return
to places that we knew (when dreams were real). We might just try
to let those deadlines die; we might remember how to feel.

Bereft of hands to hold, could we connect across the ether,
soul to soul, the heart's core impulse interlaced between
the letters on the screen?

We have not crashed, the hard drive is intact. We listen,
truly listen, to the forest: a courageous act. We draw
our power from unseen sources, and we sing
across the oceans, and your harmony
reverberates together with my melody.
I may not see your face, but are we @someplace
where Stories might begin?
Then let the spiral spin.

3am down
dee b parker

this morning i was falling
down upon my knees
3am i'm down again help me please
getting up i fill my cup
with denial despair and defeat
fill it up and drink it up and repeat
since she went away
im drowning in these man sized boots
and one, two, many shoddy mungo suits
but nothing seems to fit
doctor says you'll grow out of it
c'est au revoir to ma vie en rose
white noise and red eyed boys
trying to drown away my blues
but in my dreams my scenes have violet hues
while in my mind self hate and violence rule
it's only 3am
i'm on my knees again
i'm begging please, my friend
don't let me freeze
save me from this masquerade

my life - dee b parker, UK (she/her they/them)

would i? should i? could i?...after decades of doubt, when i finally decided to 'come out', the only essential questions that remained were when?, and who to? i was already 'out' to my best girlfriends online, and a couple of ex partners who i still remain close with, and of course a whole community on social media, but IRL i was still quietly closeted

countless opportunities came and went, Pride Days (natch), National Coming Out Days (lol), birthdays and occasions (Halloween being a particular favourite for some in the community for obvs reasons), all were considered, planned and abandoned until one particular Pride event coincided with the arrival of my first batch of patches and another frustrating lunchdate with a couple of 'the boys' in the band...

i remember that day clearly, as i observed it from my new found clarity, they came for my famous stew, and i was hoping for a jam, but it soon descended into another day of wife-beater (Stella Artois) for the boys, destroying tinny after tinny as they watched the time trials for the next days Grand Prix on a tiny screen with tinny speakers, whilst also managing to multi-task as they (unbeknowingly) mansplained to me the need to pre-warm the oven for the Aunt Bessies (sucking eggs is next), and any attempts at deeper discussions ended with three dots and a crunching of tiny gears from the tiny box(es)...

deciding that this was not the time to open my heart yet (again) i reflected upon the 'act' i had kept up, however poorly, for so many years, acting 'like a man' that i could never be, it was all still a mystery to me, i felt like an anthropologist taking endless notes on bizarre tribal behaviours without ever getting to the root of their motivations or morals, and now, none of that even mattered...

...after a few 'yawny' hints, and during a break in the 'action', the last tinnys were drained of dregs and the boys retreated to their megascreen sportcaves for their next 'hit', whilst i, as was my habit after being in 'drag' all day with the boys, immediately got into 'my' clothes and relaxed.

i don't think anyone in the Co-op realised they were seeing the real me, dressed and made up, in broad daylight, for the first time, early that evening when i popped in to get some wine and roses, and i dont think the boys on bikes who heckled 'draggy' at me as i passed them not passing realised it was my public debut, still, i took no offence just critique, and as i sat on my favourite bench toasting a perfect sunset in a trans-tinged sky with a picnic flute of wine, i'm sure the sun winked and congratulated me on my secret soft launch, cheers m'queers

Body and mind

Kyle Warwick

A cage, a lock, a prison
Trapped inside my body
Trapped inside my mind
With psychological and physical forces we bind

My body may differ but my mind does not
My mind the only true thing, my body not

To mankind I will never owe
Never owe an apology for what I feel
Never owe an action for what I do

No shame will be thrown
No judgement will be casted
Because I am a boy, just a little different
Through life we will embrace
And hope will be built
That you accept me for me

Talk to me please

Kim

[Trigger warning: bullying, child abuse]

Talk to me please,
Don't bottle it up
Your thoughts and your feelings
Please, pour me a cup

I want to be there for you
Wipe all your tears
Hold you so close to me
Ease all your fears

I know that it hurts
When you talk of that pain
But I promise you now
It won't happen again

Don't shut yourself in
Don't push me away
'Cos no matter what happens
I am here to stay

I'm not gonna leave you
Like all of them did
It wasn't your fault
You were just a kid

They hurt you so bad
Made you want to die
When I think of this
It just makes me cry

I wish I had been there
To shield you from them
But you shut me out
Wouldn't let me come in

I'm here for you now
And I won't go away
I promise you baby
I am here to stay

So talk to me please,
Don't bottle it up
your thoughts and your feelings
Please, pour me a cup

Out and Proud and Loud
Ezra May

Some people wish I was quieter

More subtle

Didn't shove it in their face

Didn't make a big deal about it

Didn't talk about it all the time

But maybe there's a reason I'm so verbally out and proud

I'm shouting to be seen

I'm begging you to hear me

But what you fail to see

What inconveniences you

Hurts me

And I'm tired of hurting invisibly

Standing in the Gents' Loos

Red Fraggle / Beck Alsford

[Trigger warning: genitals]

Standing in the Gents' loos,
Without a cock,
What does it matter?
The cubicle's locked.
Close minded arseholes,
Can't you see?
I just need a wee.
I'll close my eyes,
Stare at the floor,
Your willy's safe from me.
On the throne,
All alone,
I sit and wonder why ay, ay oh why,
You're in a stew
Over where I poo.

Feminine Inner Dialogue
Bingo Allison

I am beauty, I am grace.

But have you seen your Face?

My face is a perfect ledger of my life's journey and such

Don't Touch it! You'll smudge it! Don't fucking touch!

Seated I survey from my throne like a queen.

Adjust your knee-length skirt, your thighs might be seen!

My posture it is stately with a relaxed and settled air

Don't look up, they might see your face. Quick! Move your hair!

My eyes shine brightly with the light of everywhere I've looked

But are you sure you're properly tucked and plucked?

I float down the street entrancing every passer-by.

Head down! Lower! Don't you dare let them catch your eye.

In every conversation I amuse and entertain.

Keep your voice quiet and feminine.

Hide your interests and your brain.

I am beauty, I am grace.

You are what?

I am beauty, I am grace.

You are not!

Enough!

Enough of taking time to readjust and preen

Enough of every action being played out to be seen

Enough of silence

Enough of performing

Enough of pretence

Enough of pretending

Enough of not being able to scratch or rub my face

Enough of beauty

Enough of grace

Femme and Fuck You

Quenby Harley

[Trigger warning: genitals]

Yes I'm wearing a skirt
No, it's not a costume
Why is that your business?
Yeah I'm femme, fuck you

Yes I see you staring
Pointing, whispering, laughing, hating
You don't hide your thoughts as well as you think
Yeah I'm femme, fuck you

Yes I have a cock
What gives you the right to ask?
You're not entitled to know my body
Yeah I'm femme, fuck you

Yes I have a beard
And red lips, and purple nails
Don't really care if you think that's weird
Yeah I'm femme, fuck you

Yes I'm wearing a cute top
No that's not an invitation
I have a right to boundaries
Yeah I'm femme, fuck you

Then I meet people who open their hearts
Who don't care how I dress
Who see me as the person I am
Yeah I'm femme, fuck me?

White Noise
Kei Patrick

The best weather is   when it rains,
     inside,   at night,

     a storm,   white noise
     pouring   in the brain,

 white noise   pouring me
 into silence,   into sleep.

           It's simple.

It helps   when no real rain will fall
listening to it all   I can hear the geometry

I find I lose myself   in those parallel lines
easily   …but

but teach me   can you teach me
    how   to really cry?

       I want to learn

     To cry   I need
     I need   to let go

  somebody   to just sit
  to listen   until I am done

       crying.

Coping
RKP

[Trigger warning: abuse, violence, self-harm]

My retreat is silence - A one way violence,
Anxious intestinal snakes that slither'n'whisper mutterings of...
"Help me........please?"
Like the paint'n'words, I puke,
Fracturing fear regurgitates, wrenching,
Comes in waves, rising, through this throat.
Not to Gods or friends,
But to a Mother;

...Who might not be there...

Got soul, but where does it go after?
Cos I can't feel you anymore.
Only a cliché pain no mans land as long as Bible spines.
Dodging shadowy puddles 20:20 with a crick in my neck -
Keep lookin',
Keep lookin over unsure shoulders,
Tired'n'sittin' in the corner rockin' chaos rhythm - the disorder.
Skinnin' up with bottom'o'the bag rizla biro stains to taste...
ink the atoms and breathe,   in
Shaking...

Rearrange these particles to summit presentable -
She always said "if you ain't got nothing nice to say,
don't say nuttin' at all."
Scruffy'n'feral,
Uncontained to be containable,
Desperate to be unemotional...

Suckin' so hard on this tongue till it bleeds
wiv hopes of teachin' it a lesson.
See ma wisdom teef got rotten'n'crumbled -
Removable.
Easily disposable'n'wary of those that call themselves family.
Trust is a hard thing to come by nowadays.

I want to abandon the theme...
Where you leave me.

Bang these bones - Xylophone -
into bruises changing...
Blood blotted skins,
Petrol coloured Mood rings -
Shades that settle in UV spectrums,
Self Portrait Rorschach tests,
With scars once affectionately named, "noughts'n'crosses."

They are medals of battles I...have...won...
Self made but this body a crime scene - so fuck the doll!
I'll show ya where HE dragged me by the neck'n'mum watched
passively after with'a son on her waist,
Four years apart - A second chance to be a father.
Discipline love measured in welts'n'a foot to trip'ya,
Counting down,
10, 9, 8...before they drew out the spatula.
The drawer'n'smack on the counter -
Fear controller.

I'm Tryin' hard to forgive those who trespassed,
Triggered flashbacks inside this skull - brain cinematics,
Hands drawing close without invitation..
Using bodies to break boundaries
Ignoring those lined limb limitations
redder than the depths of Medusa's Lake.
Progress really ain't linear, but I promise you
I am,
I am,
I am gettin better.

Believe in Me (lyrics)
Elliott Boot

I don't know where I'm going yet
I know I can't be scared of what comes next
I need to see
That you believe in me

I try to keep my emotions at bay
Sometimes they spill over, try as I may
I need to see
That you believe in me

This is me trying again
This is me starting again
I need you to believe in me my friend
I need to believe in me again

I know you want to see me win
I can't believe you've stuck with me through thick and thin
But I need to see
You still believe in me

This is me trying again
This is me starting again
I need you to believe in me my friend
I need to believe in me again

The time is here and now
If I choose to take it
I'm gonna sing loud and proud
I hope I don't waste it
Can you hear me now?
This is my time

This is me trying again
This is me starting again
I need you to believe in me my friend
I need to believe in me again

This is me trying again
This is me starting again
I need you to believe in me my friend
I need to believe in me again
I need to believe in me again
I need to believe in me again

Questions for cis people
Joey White

[Trigger warning: genitals, sexual abuse, anti-trans violence]

Cis people,
I'm right here, so why is my existence confusing?
Why am I in the same box as mermaid, dragon, pixie and griffin?
If seeing is believe me and you can see me, surely I exist and
if I were fictional I would be going to much better parties.
Why would I talk to people who question my existence when I could
go hang out in Dracula's castle anyway?

Cis people,
Why are you cis?
But… why? Why would you want to be?
Same reason as why I'm trans.

Cis people,
Have you had, you know, the surgery? The cis surgery?
There isn't one?
Then stop asking me if I have had 'the op' yet.
I don't know which operation you mean!
I mean, I had my tonsils out when I was nine.
Do tonsils or lack thereof decide my gender for me?
Or can I be trusted to do that myself?

Cis people,
Let me get this straight. Do you ask everyone about their genitals?
Do you measure how much of a manly man your cis male friends are
by asking exactly how large their dicks are?
If they're circumcised or not?
How low their balls hang?

If that strikes you as a little awkward,
it's awkward for me too.

Cis people,
Why do you think you have the right to touch me?
Being trans is not an invite to grab and squeeze
and see what's real and what's not
as if I'm a free-for-all exhibit
instead of a human being.

Cis people,
Why do you feel the need to inform me that I 'look like a girl'?
Why do you roll your eyes when I tell you to call me 'he'?
Why do you feel the need to inform me
 you'll 'have to get used to' calling me 'he'?
Why must you act as if my existence is exhausting for you,
as if it isn't for me?
Every 'she' and eye-roll and huff
is just another punch to my wellbeing
causing bruises upon bruises that you cannot see
doesn't even matter.
Another reminder of how inconvenient our existence is.
"It's fine," I say. "Happens all the time."
It shouldn't.
It's not that hard to change a pronoun.

Cis people,
You create a world
where nearly half of transgender youths
feel they are no longer welcome, and think death is preferable.
So excuse me if I don't apologise
for your hand stinging when you slap me.

I'm not going to beg for forgiveness for bleeding on you
when you slice my whole being in two
and like hell am I going to set myself on fire to keep you warm.

Because every transgender, genderqueer, genderfluid and non-binary
brother, sister and sibling I have
that have seen the afterlife as some glowing exit sign
from a place where they're not really wanted.

Trans people,
You are wanted.
You are not inconvenient.
I'm sorry it hurts, I know it does.
But you don't need to apologise for your existence
when they misgender you.
Be as loud and as angry and as bright and vibrant as you need
for them to get the message that you are here to stay,
whether they damn well like it or not.

Cis people,
Did you know that there are more colours than pink and blue?

My Life – Joey White, UK (he/him)

[Trigger warning: transphobia, fatphobia, violence, sexual assault, attempted suicide]

Diary of a trans fat kid

Age 6 I ask my mother what we're having for dinner. "Air for you" she replied. "You could do with skipping a meal."

Age 7 my mother lights a cigarette and tells me not to start smoking as our family has an addictive personality. I say I'm not addicted to anything. "Yes you are," she says and pokes my belly. "Food." It was the first time I ever felt guilty for eating.

Age 8 I'm still trying to learn how to tie my shoes. My grandmother scolds me I put my foot up on my knee to tie it. I struggle to lean down and she screams that I can't tie my shoes because I'm so fat. I'm disciplined for crying. It's my fault, she tells me.

Age 9 at the kids club at the playground. All I want to do is play on the swings and a group of teenage boys ask where my vagina is. Every second I wait for my dad's car to come and pick me up feels like a lifetime as they shout at me how they would get over the difficulties of the puppy fat around my belly to fuck me. They're angry when I don't answer their questions about my vagina. "Do you even have a pussy? Is your pussy fat too? Is it even fuckable?"

Age 11 I enter secondary school bright eyed and full of hope for the future, ignorant of what was to come. I quickly learn that in order to get home safely I have to run home the second the bell rings or wait in the toilets for fifteen minutes before walking home. If I don't, I go home with bruises. It's not cool to punch a kid three years younger than you, unless they're fat. Then it's hilarious. I start cutting myself regularly, and go on a vegetable only diet as the most nutritional food a fat kid can have throughout the day is half a carrot and a tin of sweetcorn.

Age 11 at an anti-bullying assembly we're told it's wrong to make fun of others for things they cannot control. I am told I will stop suffering violence if I just lose weight.

Age 12 whilst dealing with the loss of my mother I also listen to the accusations that I'm lying. I learn that tragedy never happens to fat kids because they lie as a way to get attention because they are incapable of getting positive attention for anything they do.

Age 12 they stick pins in me to see if I pop. They're shocked I bleed. They pin me down and whip me to see how much my skin wobbles and are shocked when it splits open.

Age 12, two packets of paracetamol before bed, followed by violent sickness. Fat kid couldn't even die right.

Age 13 in an attempt to seem as cishet as possible I write a note to a boy asking if he wants to be my boyfriend. In front of the whole class he stands up and shouts that I need to get some liposuction first. I realise nobody will ever consider me beautiful.

Age 13 I'm pushed down the stairs to see if I would roll, as they laughed I went to hospital with a damaged wrist and a sling for the next week.

Age 14 I go to the doctor for a verruca on my foot. He frowns at me and tells me that I'm so fat it would make no difference if I stopped eating altogether. My body would have enough to live on. I pretend to eat healthily, but I go by the doctor's advice and do not eat at all. After a week I eat some cucumber and hate myself for it. The intensity of my attempt lead to a dislocated knee. The crutches were another reason to laugh at me. Even my legs can't handle all my fat, they said.

Age 15 I discover there is nothing funnier than the sexualisation of a fat person. For the next few years I learn that having my behind grabbed, squeezed, slapped and punched is going to be part and parcel of everyday life. When it stopped being a novelty for some, they would try to hit as hard as possible, using weapons if they could. My chest was grabbed and groped and touched as sexual assault became just a daily routine. It didn't count, I thought. We were told that sexual assault only occurred when desire became so much they couldn't resist – but nobody wanted me. They did it because nobody wanted me. How could it possibly be sexual assault?

Age 16 I came out as the man I am, a few terrified, wobbly footsteps into manhood. "You only feel that way because you are fat", said the doctor. "If you lose weight, you will see you are pretty and you will no longer want to be a man."

Age 17 I am told that straight boys do not want a fat girl, and gay boys will not be tempted by some fat girl pretending she is a boy.

Age 19 I feel my crotch grabbed by someone who is supposed to be my friend, and told the fat cannot make up for my manhood that is lacking.

Diary of a trans fat adult.

Age ongoing. Today I am stronger than I ever have been.

Today I am far more than anything they told me I was.

Today I fight for the fat kids and the trans kids that do not deserve what happened to me.

Today I am still fat.

Today I am still trans.

Today, I am happy.

Destination
Dalton Harrison

The story starts,
Where you choose to enter,
I lost my way,
But found redemption,
Not sure when,
Like children listening,
To nursery rhymes designed to link laurels with their morals,
What's mine?
Wagon rides on sweat,
Out of breath,
Timed dinners,
Poor discussions,
I wake up in nightmares sweat,
To reconnect with the space,
I left,
At empty chairs at dinner tables,
In cinema queues,
On bar stools and fancy restaurants,
My family roots got broken,
The seed of stems,
Trying to regrow,
I found a way to re-pot,
Re-ponder and redirect my destination,
To separate the darkness,
In me,
To look up out of all I knew,
To move forward
To find the light.

The Trans Revolution
Paula Adrianne

[Trigger warning: anti-trans violence]

We wanted to be left alone,
to be our real true selves,
but that didn't work for you,
You made our lives a living hell

It's quite dangerous being trans,
We live our lives in fear,
Thousands of us are assaulted
and hundreds killed every year

Many trans folk hide away
and live their lives in stealth
they're not being true to who they are,
and it's bad for mental health

There are bigots all around us,
Including Boris J,
But the revolutions coming,
The bigots are going to pay

You may beat us individually,
but we number quite a few,
and together with our allies,
We'll take the fight to you

It's not too late to make amends,
Stop your wicked ways,
Stop bullying folk because,
They're brown or trans or gay!

I am my own mirror
Purity K Paige

I am my own mirror.
I speak good things n compliments
to and about myself
usually regardless of the situations,

I tell myself that the future holds
better opportunities and better plans for me,

I smile through pain
but tell the girl I see in the mirror
that there will be more to life,
there will be great breakthroughs,
great endeavors
and there will be that time
for the long awaited freedom that I deserved

My brokeneness, my struggles,
my trials and tribulations etc
will still always find me ready to strive
and looking forward to a very bright future to come
that I deserve and deserved many years ago.

I am my own mirror
n what i see in the mirror
is a beautiful soul that deserves better

I tell this girl that we will be better one day
and ashame the devil
and we will always strive to be better
with honesty and being true to us.

Patience pays, situations change,
I mean a lot changes with time,
who one saw as a nobody
might turn out a somebody
so be slow to judge but more kind
as in be too slow to judge n more kind
n probably slower
because life can turn around actually,
Such is life.

#iam #my #own #mirror.

Triptorelin Time
Autumn Barkley

The needle enters, its contents left
A euphoria found in a leaky tap
Formed of muscle, found as pain
And yet, an anticlimax, as if another day

4 years, 4 f#@%!?g years
Paperwork mistakes drawn on my canvas
Lazy work with careless consequence
Discrimination by any name besides

First, the courage to speak my truth
Then, the strength to endure abuse
Next, the rage to strike back for our youth
And now? Unlike a pulling tooth

There is no pain left but aches
a groaning, creaking of my body
no wait, no fear (or not as much)
and yet my reflection alters little

A noticeboard of cautionary tales
A form aged in denial of ourselves
Unlike fine wine this cannot improve
We will drown sorrows in each other

And yet! and still! There is (a) little change!
My fire dimmed, my place assured
Comfort unwanted, unnecessary
What of all those I left behind?

The younger me would hate my speed
"Rattle down their doors! she'd say
and yet I grow in lover's embrace
each second lost to save my past

The Fear of Transition

Jay Rose Ana

Before I transitioned,
There were a couple of things, I admit I envisioned.
Thoughts that ran through my head, and through my heart,
Whilst I was driving or in bed, my soul, kept me up at night.
Not feeling whole, forcing heart and mind apart.

I will try and number them in a list,
It is not a big list, so please persist.
And if you do feel, the temptation to resist,
Then that is okay, I am not going to insist.

Number one, will my family stop loving me? That is a big one to start
with! Do you agree?

Number two, will the world hate me or accept me? Will it let me be?

Number three, will people I call friend, walk away from me? It is a
possibility.

Number four, will anyone hold a friendly hand out to me? Or will I
walk alone, just me, eternally?

Number five, why I am doing this? What is in it for you? And what's
in it for me? I have new hopes for number three.

Number six, am I ill? Have I lost my mind? Is there something the
matter with me? Do I have the right to be free? Me?

I said it was a short list, those are the big hitters,
The ones that question my right to exist.
And those like, will I ever be kissed?
You know the ones, the ones you whisper quietly,
When you think you are alone,
Or getting ready, in a mirror, when your cover is blown.
When you whisper to your soul and it reassures to you.

Number one was easy, they still love me, that one was silly really. But
that is just me. Maybe I was lucky, for some people, this list stops
here. And they live in a world of fear. Do not hide away, there is
always a friend near.

Number two, is a maybe, it is a weird and sometimes frightening world out there, but it also fabulous and miraculous and I sometimes wonder, what will today be?

Number three, most definitely. Enough said. Let us do four instead.

Number four, I have had more hugs than at any other time in my life. Every hug I get feeds my soul, makes me feel whole. For that alone, I would enrol.

Number five, because this is who I am, and I am not afraid anymore. I am being true to myself through every single pore. It never gets easier but now I trust my core, and I will endure, of that you can be very sure.

Number six, I think I am about the same as most other people, if this were a game. So, I think that means I might be doing okay. At least today. I haven't thought about throwing my life away, in the past few days, anyway.

So, transitioning went this way,
The sun shone, like it always does.
I felt it shined on me, briefly, but the Sun is busy,
It has a whole galaxy to illuminate,
And a billion stars in the sky to set free.
There was no massive spotlight, not on me.
I am just trying to do my best.
Getting through each day.
No presentations, or congratulatory speeches.
No secret, just acceptance, of what life teaches.

She's Trans, Don't Panic!

Jay Rose Ana

She is trans, DON'T PANIC!

She didn't beam down from another planet!
Anyway, Mercury is too far away,
And Mars and Venus,
Have their own problems, don't they?

But let me tell you, that this woman shines!
Oh, she shines, like a firefly, and why!?
Because she has found the answer!
The answer to that ultimate question.

No, not 42! That would never do!

The question is rhetorical, "I know who I am?"
The ultimate quest, we all live to pursue.
The one precious thing, a metaphorical ring.
It fuels her soul, carries her through.

Her days are not easy, that is a different truth.
But really, how easy, was your day for you?

So, DON'T PANIC! Stay calm!
Laser set to stun; she won't do you any harm.
You may get a friendly smile,
Not a close encounter.
Maybe a subtle glance, under the counter.

Or not, she is just going about her day.
Like you, in pretty much the same, ordinary, way.

The only thing that really makes her stand out,
Except being totally fabulous of course,
Is trusting who she feels she is, on the inside.

And wearing it, on her outside.
Of her closet, and her world,
And her body, and her soul.
And that is what really makes her whole.

She likes watching science fiction shows,
And reality television.
Reading fantasy stories,
And meeting up with friends, watching Eurovision!

Not that we can get out much during lockdown.
But eventually, that will end,
And she can have a cold glass of something,
With someone she holds dear, maybe a friend.

She is not a hitchhiker; she has no magic spells.
She has no special Doctor, who can
Explain all the technical words you use to describe her.

Or make sense of all the changes, her heart compels.

And yet, today, she made it, out of her own front door.
You go girl! You pioneer!
Off to face the real world, once again!!
We are right behind you! Or at least, fairly near.

The question is, will she make it back home safely?

Fact over fiction.
Hate over fact.

In a world of non-fiction,
The odds are stacked against her.
Watch the news reports this evening.
The statistics are not good.
Trans hate is pretty convincing.

Already, this year, in the US alone,
The number of trans people murdered,
Exceeded last years toll.
In just seven months.
And for most of that time,
Weren't we all at home?

Safe and sound, in the security of lock down.
Danger lurks, hate smirks,
Challenging her right to endure.
And this, for her,
Is the only thing for sure.

DON'T PANIC!

She's Trans.

(Written in 2020, during the COVID-19 pandemic lockdown)

My Life – Jay Rose Ana, UK (she/her)

The night I cried in a service station car park

In October 2018, I was driving home on the motorway on a long commute from work. I was a man. It was a dark rainy Friday evening, when out of the blue I started to cry, uncontrollable tears. I pulled into the motorway service station and had to get out of my car and I cried in the rain. I cried for a very long time.

These were happy tears, tears of joy, honestly I felt like dancing, because on that particular drive home, I had experienced a life changing moment of clarity, a realisation, where my life, my whole-self, actually made sense for the very first time.

I was misgendered.

I had been living over fourty years labelled as a man. I was happy to be considered male, reasonably successful, I had a long time partner, and I am a father of three, but, with the benefit of hindsight, there was, I believe, a sense of not quite fitting in somehow but, I never thought of that as trans, and so I pushed that aside early on because that was the safest thing to do. So, I had "no prior experience" of trans.

My earliest memory was being at infant school in the West Midlands and at playtime children labelled boys and children labelled girls were separated into different playgrounds with a huge white line down the middle, that line is still there today. I used to walk along that white line curious about what was happening over in that other space, as it felt like it was a place I should be, I was drawn to it.

That soon stopped because adults, at that time and in that place, had a simpler understanding of gender, and kids in the playground were constantly reinforced with those messages and stereotypes. Kids labelled boys did these kinds of things. Kids labelled girls did those kinds of things.

I ended up being bulled quite a bit, I always stood my ground, but I soon learned to forget about those ideas, I was probably only six or seven years old back then, and over time I forgot about them.

I became introverted, shy, and a bit of a dreamer I suppose.

I should also say that I didn't speak at all until I was eleven years old, childhood had not been kind. I made unrecognisable sounds sometimes, at infant school they put this down to shyness and kind of ignored it. I had a lot of speech therapy during secondary school, and that was all down to just one teacher, who for some reason, invested their own time in me, early on.

She helped me with so many things and she is a really good example for people who think that one person can't make a difference, you can.

But I often look back at that night, there in the motorway services, as the first point where I feel I really transitioned, and from that moment on I was ready to transition immediately.

However, the next real-world step for me was taking time to really consider and accept personal transition for myself, but also how my transition would impact my immediate family.

Acceptance of personal gender transition

When I got home that night it was very late, but I wanted to wake everyone up and tell them the amazing thing I had realised about myself. But I didn't. I let them sleep.

Instead, I sat on the idea for a couple of weeks, because, even though, personally, I was comfortable with it, I was aware of transphobic behaviours, you know, people who hate transgender, as there is quite a bit of misunderstanding over what it means. The one thing I was fully aware of was that the impact of negative behaviours would not just be towards me but towards my family too.

I made time to think and really consider it, then the day came for me to talk to my partner and tell her how I feel and to share the realisation I had had.

She listened intently, and when I was done, I thought that's the end of that but she surprised me. She thought about it for a while longer then agreed it was the right thing to do, for me, and she hugged me, and held me, and she has stood by my side ever since, even though we are no longer together as ultimately, she married a man.

I had professional counselling from two different counsellors. Then I had to tell my children, and that was the thing I feared most. They surprised me too. Our children have been pretty amazing actually, and said they thought it was cool, which reassures me a) we have not done a terrible job in helping them grow up so far and b) the world is changing, and they are a lot better prepared for it than I ever was.

The next part of my transition involved reaching out further beyond personal transition to work and friends. Explaining my situation to people has been a challenge for me personally; and it does not get easier over time, every time feels like the first time. Lockdown has introduced more times when we meet people for the first time, often over video calls, which can be uncomfortable for some as, for me, I find it helps to talk to a person face to face, in person.

I have talked to many people on a 1-2-1 basis and each has had its challenges and let me tell you, people will surprise you. People who I imagined would be supportive were shocked and horrified and ran for the hills whilst people I expected the worst from were often the ones who gave me a reassuring hug and became closer to me.

Emerging as someone labelled transgender there is a huge amount of "look confident" at play when inside I am often shaking. Early on, I could never find quite the right words to concisely, or eloquently, explain my experience in a way that feels entirely comfortable to me. It is not quite the same as, say, a house move, or getting a new car, or planning a holiday.

Some negative people saw that as an opportunity to berate me or consider me "not really trans" but you know there is no one-way of being "trans", we are all different, at different points in transition, and have different goals. Also, not everyone who transitions gender considers themselves trans, that is something that people generally assume and put on you, like a label, or a heavy coat.

I have to say, the majority of people I have talked to have been completely supportive and fabulous, and that really helps me get through the day, with confidence, and shows how great people really are. And they far outnumber the people who have been negative, so I acknowledge the negativity happens, but I accept it, let it go, and focus on the positivity instead.

I, Human (lyrics)
The Bleeding Obvious

Teach me to hate myself as much as you hate me.
My thoughts have no gender, my consciousness no form.
Similarities make the difference, I am free to not consume.
There is nothing to tolerate. Jump up and be reborn.

Acceptance is to peace when you delete the media scrub.
Careers forged from blind words, exfoliate your mind.
Free to be a person. Germination from constraint.
Dignity. Integrity. Nobility and Pride.

Humans learn from childhood the rules of subjugation.
Break the rule of rules. Liberation of humankind.
Shatter the bonds of autonomy. Revise your definitions.
My priorities, my values, my fate. Mine.

Powerless we're isolated, repressed we are joyless
Assign the human eunuch's bond, the business of fear again.
Embrace difference and similarity, we all hurt and bleed.
We all feel and love, choose not to be enraged.

Male. Female. Him. Her. Untick that box, it's defective.
Your ideals are solely yours, unlabelled we're the same.
Words of violence. Words that kill. Innocent and deadly.
They are your own invention and the basis of your shame.

A life begins, we're all human….A life ends, we're all human.
Isn't it bleedin' obvious?

Lyrics from the debut album *The Bleeding Obvious,* reproduced with the
permission of the artist. https://bleedingobvious.uk/debut/lyrics

Normalised

Eden Irving

'Normal' is a man-made term,
circulating and suffocating the existence of difference.
Normality in moronity of society's conformity
as every day a heightened minority's mortality rates rise
with iron-clad facts and unaddressed bloodshed.
Footnotes in lie-drenched news outlets.
'Normal' is their anti-slur –
anything else seen as an affront to the norm.

Man-made commodity, an oddity.
Quality of character questioned whenever a toxic stance is challenged
and those sick of being sat and talked down to take a stand.
I want 'Hindsight's a Bitch' engraved on my headstone.
What is 'normal'? Mine – is it yours? Might you lend it for a day?
There isn't enough time, enough millimetres on the sundial,
to make a dent in this question.

I sever safety lines and dive deeper, mining away at my peace of mind.
Lessons of life hacks, finance advice and customer service skills
never tell you how to get your head
out of the gravel of your glue-coated pastime.
Sticking to the words of a half-forgotten backstory.
Cry me a bath to wash away this dark sinful interior,
to soak, dry and smell plainly of clarity for the first time.
Body hair fields grow a plenty,
ones I wish would shrivel, die and be shat upon by weed killer.
Keeping up appearances
as you mow down your personality's willows and weeds;
trimmed to match perfected lawns surrounding your lot in life.
Never mind the death tainting your back-yard patio.

Once more I start itching, bitching,
at the dreaded itch of long-sewn stitching,
unravelling via travelling a subconscious glitching;
sanity lost to a collective hivemind.
Ambiguous androgyny stolen for eternity.
Didn't see what you saw worth loving until you requested a refund.
Five stages of grief encapsulated in memory foam
as I cry myself to sleep
in a graveyard of gender expression.
The in-between of a suit and a dress – so, stress?

But I'll never get down life's yellow brick road
if I spend all my self-esteem re-laying the tarmac
to ease other's travels.
I can better pull brethren to solid ground once I find my own footing.

We've accepted 'normal' as painful,
the be all and end all of tribulations and trials.
Let 'normal' be struck from the record.
Let 'normal' be overhauled from the ground up.
Let 'normal' be filled with bad puns and observations;
watching Bi-planes overhead, doing Aro-bics,
completing Trans-actions with Binary numbers
for your banker's Queer-ies,
browsing the Pan-try as I AM ABout to cook A FABulous cake!
Everyone's obsessed with being 'normal'…
but who's proud to be it?

Though a Princess, he is Nothing
L. Cable

What's a boy to do
When he can't save his own life?

Panzer man,
Or trophy wife?

They tell me Princess Die
On your knees, take my tongue and fly.

My jewellery on the floor,
Now the whole world knows I'm not normal anymore.

I wish one of us was wrong,
Or that I could be strong in the way you want.

Undressing my glamour
Trade my pearls for armour.

Lead me to self-doubt, path gaslit,
Follow your fingers, make me a prince when I lie like this.

If I fall alone, the princess dies,
Then alone forever him and I.

The devil and I; he sits on my shoulder,
I will go to hell if here is colder.

Go back to the country,
I'll go back to being me.

Cut my hair in my sleep,
Kill the company I keep.

Say it to me,
Just accept that you are lonely.

I get no sleep, have no tongue
But the arms to hold and the legs to run

To any other man to make me feel like his son.
So, I push, while you cut,

With the lights purple around me.
Exactly how many ways can you quiet me?

And we go hard, follow the arrow where it lands:
I rise, where is your proof that I'm a man?

I go hard, the princess dies,
On your knees, pass my pearls and fly.

Gather my gowns, call me a taxi:
Have not the rights for a king so happy.

I could never be a knight, with a sword on my hip
For mine is the crown that's hardest to slip.

Bad Side

Aidan Sarson

Sometimes when I'm depressed
The bad side takes control
He's a nasty little fucker
In fact, a complete arsehole.

He doesn't care that I love you
Or that you mean the world to me
He'll still try to push you away
Try to hurt you, so that hurts me

I knew when I wrote that text
It was something I shouldn't do
He convinced me it was appropriate
But I knew it would upset you

I'm sorry that you met him
I try to keep him subdued
He's a side of me I do not like
But present when I'm in a mood

I can't say you won't see him again
I'm afraid that wouldn't be true
But I'll try to keep a lid on it
And not let him win through.

The Butterfly, my metamorphosis

Chrissie Chevasutt

It seemed like only yesterday
my young daughter
took me by the hand
led me
out the door.

"We are going to look
for butterflies."

A long, deep, profound
child silence.

"Where do the butterflies live?"

I strapped her in her kiddy seat,
she looked regal as the queen.
She hummed and sang
this summers day
as we drove
to where my father's ashes lay
scattered over these hills

I remembered as if it was yesterday
how he had gambolled and galloped
after butterflies
on these grassy slopes
capturing them
a moment in time
with his camera

or he'd stoop in wonder

close to tears
to marvel at some rare orchid
and he'd swear me to secrecy
of his sacred sect
'preservers of the mystery'
but I only wanted
the ice cream
at the other end
of our walk

so here I am today
my daughter marches me
triumphantly
we climb the stile
sit on the fence
munch on our oatcakes
watch the cows
swishing flies
with tails
they turn
and smile

everyone
everything
seems to smile for my daughter
even the view
the sky

off she skips
laughing
down the hill

"Look, look, look!"
"Come quickly!"

"I've seen a butterfly!"
(surprise, surprise)

My father knew his butterflies
where to find them
and when

"Isn't it beautiful
like a fairy?"
"What kind of butterfly is it?"
"Oh look!
another one!"

"That's a *Polyommatus coridon*."

She's already gone

"A polywhattus oridon?"

"A Chalk Hill Blue."

"I love love love these chalkyblues."

Her breath is taken away
spell bound
enchanted as they flutter gently
floats ascends
soars away
caught on the light breeze
of warm air rising
from the river in the valley
below
she dances after it
 We lie on our backs
staring into the sky
skylarks sing

tumble
their music
fills our cathedral
as we bow down in worship
and all is tranquil
time stops
stands still
for us now
heaven falls

we wonder at the frail vulnerable beauty
of these ethereal creatures
noiseless
silent
spirit like
here for a fleeting moment
to dazzle
enchant
ablaze
beguiled
by their mystery

the long deep silence of a searching mind

"Where do butterflies come from?"

"Come on, let me show you."

How could she know?
Just how?
How could she know
I asked my father that same question
as we lay on our backs
side by side

staring into the sky
watching skylarks dance and trill
pirouette and fall
time stands still
and I am lost
in mystery and wonder

we wander and we wonder
not so far
into a blaze of colour
patches of delicate
small yellow flowers
densely packed together

these flowers litter the ground
across the fields flung

"Ssssh"

I bend down slowly
on my knees
in prayer
like my father before me
hoping
hoping
she sits down quietly
sensing a moment unfolding

Horseshoe vetch
Hippocrepis comosa

succulent food for the caterpillar of the
Chalk Hill Blue

my father's favourite butterfly
it's mine too
so delicate soft
so feminine
tail dusted with pale dusky spots
wings traced with white lace
an otherworldly sublime messenger
of life's
short and temporary nature
here today
gone tomorrow

I lift a leaf
we peer underneath
small pale dots
perfect spheres
clustered together

"Ooh, what are those?"

"They are butterfly eggs."

"They're so teeny weeny tiny winy!"
"How do they get from that tiny little egg with their big wings?
It must be awful difficult!"

"Come and have a look..."

We crawl off on all fours

I find one, two, three...
four and more
"Uurggh!"
"Yuk!"

"Creepy crawlies!"
"They're not butterflies!"
She looks in disdain, nose wrinkled up in mock disgust.
"They're just for boys,
boys laugh at them,
hide them
in our bags at school,
they tried to put one down my neck!"
"Yuk yuk yuk!"

These ugly
repulsive fellows
like hairy maggots
obsessed with eating
in the few short weeks
of their drab existence
they grow in body weight a thousand times
discarding skin like clothes
several times
dragging round their gorged bodies
they even have eyes and hazard warning yellow lines
painted on their backs
to scare away the predators

"I don't even want to touch one!"

"Trust me, I know just how you feel."

"I don't want to look at these,
where have the butterflies gone?"

"These are butterflies."

She stares at me now

incredulous
jaw dropped
"no!
stop teasing me."

"Yes, really they are."

"Oh my golly goodness gosh, not really?"

She looks at me, unsure,
she thinks I'm joking.

"Come on then, let's go find some more butterflies."

We chase butterflies
and fall exhausted in a heap
munching on huge slabs
of cake
sipping on water
lying on our backs
in the warmth of summer's sun
clouds tower into eternity
light pours visions
of nature's glories
I tell dad's story

"Like all butterflies, the Chalk Hill Blue
can only lay its eggs on one particular type of plant, in this case,
horseshoe vetch, it's the only food its caterpillars can eat.
Dozens of tiny eggs
laid on the underside of the leaves,
protected from the rain and birds,
soaked in the rays of summer sun
these eggs hatch into tiny, almost microscopic caterpillars

all they do whilst they are alive
is eat
(truly carnal earthly creatures)."
"Yuk, yuk, yuk...
uuurgh"
"So how can a caterpillar be a butterfly?"

"Well it's not really."

"But you said it was?"

She knows there is a story unfolding
a revelation
a science
a discovery,
she licks her lips
anticipation
she is at four
already wise

"Now the caterpillar has grown so fat,"
my father continues,

"He climbs under a leaf and starts to weave a cocoon,
if he were a certain type of moth, that cocoon would be spun in silk.
Silk, the most beautiful material on earth.
Soon the caterpillar has locked himself in his own tomb."

"What's a tomb?"

"A tomb is where they put dead people."

"Is the caterpillar dead?"

"No, not really."

"How can he breathe?"

She's lost in wonder
at the power of the story
so am I

"What is happening?"

I am lost for the words
how to explain to my daughter,
so I carry on with grown up words
my father's words
I hope they will suffice

"What is happening is one of the most incredible metamorphosis
known on earth,
in this dark place
the caterpillar starts to change,
muscles, sinews,
tendons, wings
start to form
In his decaying body
parts of the caterpillar die,
legs and body wither
in a kind of soup,
a liquid living gloop."

"Eeeewh
blurgh"

"Yes, the caterpillar sort of eats itself, dissolving
releasing enzymes
that turn its body into a kind of mush"

I'm watching her
and listening to my father
her eyes are buzzing
filled with light and fear and wonder

at the magic,
mystery and wonder
quite the most terrifying story she's yet been told

"So within this soup
this metamorphosing body
are memory cells that start to feed on the protein rich liquid womb
and grow
into wings, legs, antenna and eyes
what started as maybe fifty cells
could soon be fifty thousand
so in this tomb
this place of utter darkness
total constriction
unable to move
the butterfly is formed,
but she can't get out"

"could we help her?"

"How do you mean?"

"You know,
cut the tomb open,
with one of your work knives,
you know,
set her free,
so she could fly off
up into the sky
with all the other butterflies
and be happy
and free?"

"No, that would kill her."

"So what must she have to do to escape the dark tomb?"

"For days and days and days
all she can do
is struggle
even to move just a teeny muscle

almost crushed, suffocated
as her wings grow beautiful
and threaten to crush her little body
she wriggles and writhes
stretches and flexes."

"Like mummy doing yoga?"

"A bit, but more like mummy
doing yoga
locked in a wheelie bin."

"That must be truly horrible!"

"Yes, maybe, but all this struggle is making her strong, so strong,
until one day she is so strong and so beautiful
she breaks open the tomb
breaks it wide open
and if you watch carefully
you'll see her hanging there
from that leaf
as she unfurls
the first time
these wings
stretches her glory out
and shakes

quivering, shimmering
settling

warming in the light
where she belongs
for a few brief moments

a few tentative gentle whispering flaps

before she allows herself to let go
and fall

and she falls
and floats
turns
flicks her wings
in powerful strokes
catches the wind
and flies
she is up
free
incandescent
transcendent
lifted up
borne on the wind
away
where she wills."

my dad is long gone now
I look at my daughter
tears flood her eyes
gently roll down her cheeks.

This place
where Heaven kisses us.

Touched.
RKP

I'm poorly written & stained in inspiration,
Like secret sealed school notes,
Read out for humiliation,
Remembered years later with a pained blush.
Open the window'n'let out my soul;
Welcome the cold in.
Thaw out those farewells,
Cos Nothing compares,
To the sensation of her forehead when it was kissed.
Ghosts roam East Anglia - Nostalgia -
My home is ashes...
Strands of hair are relics,
Kept in OXO tins for Sunday Roasts that were never served.
Morbid keep sakes,
To keep safe,
While the rhythm of rain keeps time.
Kindness comes with suspicion'n'a flinch,
Cos hindsight's a bitch'n'sewn the seams for a loneliness
that dreams viciously,
A vintage misery barking accuracy,
Gnawing at old wounds.
She was a blade'n'i'm still paper,
Crumpling under pressure -
A gravitas equal to setting suns & ultimatums.
Relentlessness stings an emotional flesh that never surrenders,
or forgets,
These raw shredded stitches that disintegrate,
Like how the grass blows when it's cut,
But it's never greener.

Just darker...like the shadows
When that light hit their faces,
Slowly turning into my Mother's.

Why did I keep falling,
Searching in wrong places.
Should have taken a break at the apostrophe'n'dash,
Rewind when the lines got racked Quick'n'thin like mercury,
Passed out dreaming of lobotomies...
Still, I was non the wiser for knowin'.
Stay hidden in the Attic,
Lay long enough to heal'n'become floor...
Feel me as you walk.
Follow sweet Robin's song to soothe in A&E,
For shattered hearts that ain't broken,
Just tired.
Cos if I love you was a promise then they broke it rolling along
mendips.
Echoic memory of protective cries,
As emotive tornados tore through.
Urges with balled fists for hot liquids,
Blister identities essence,
Destroy everything that she ever...

Will my hands always look like hers?

On the out
Dalton Harrison

[Trigger warning: prison, suicide, drug use]

One week sees one death,

Two weeks sees four more recalls, someone o.d on the floor,
eyes so glazed like an animal stuffed in a museum hall,

A month, a girl on my floor handcuffed
and screaming in a drunk rage,
she's pushed into a van. it's a dawn raid,
A stark warning to all those who question their place back on the out,
With celebratory liquid or pill treats to mark the occasion,

The week after I am met with spitting rage by the vagrant drug dealer
that recognizes I am from the same place,
some girl swopted a rock for her phone now she needs to pay,

The week after she's not going out
and I am left walking the long way,

A day off two months and she loaned out too much,
I see recall after recall and wonder how she hung on this long,
While rehabilitated shoplifters ask me
if I want these expensive aftershaves,

two months and a day,
I replay my friend's suicide
while the voices inside her mind leave only death to snatch her away,
I watch in a daze handfuls of absconds drift out like tides,
I bump into them casually outside parks or pharmacies and jobcentres,
saying hi but looking worse for wear laughing,

But today's a tooth missing, weight loss and a black eye,
Drunk men standing nearby questioning my concerned voice,

three months and I hear they're back inside,

Doing fine just saying hi, remembering the outside
like distance memories of childhood dreams,
lost daydreams wondering how anyone makes it out there it's crazy,
while I try to remind myself that I'm doing ok,

That five months is seen with clear eyes,
Not robbed in streets by random acts,
My face beat but strangely don't call the police,

I see six months without sitting in dark dirty dens
hidden by respectable street signs,
In rooms designed to take your youth, your money and your life,

I wonder in a year if some will have made it here
without using prison as respite,
without losing their life,
without paper licenses keeping them right,

I wonder if they stand and say,
On the out is better than in here
On the out is worth all my tears

My Life – Dalton Harrison (he/him)

I have been judged my whole life. My earliest memory was fo having a Dutch mother and a English father. For being too thick. Fo failing at school. For being too tall. For looking too different.

I felt my young self grow inward. My reality was like Plato's cave: only saw the shadows of what I thought and other people's ignorance t it. A school yard then turned into a prison inside my mind. Educatio was learning how to survive, I could not catch up. I felt shame from such a young age about me. I was wrong. I was different from wha everyone else saw. I felt anger. I felt desperate. I was a victim - then wasn't.

I tried to find resilience. I found my body was my prison. My life was a prison. Then reality caught up with me. I was sentenced. Left wit a lifetime of pain in an overnight wing and a dirty cell. I had spent m life trying to please everyone one but me. Yet the me I saw I wanted t kill. The real me was a secret burden hidden deep within my ow internal prison. Stored away since the moment I was told: "it wasn't o to walk around with my shirt off, I was getting too old."

This echoed in the start of a journey where I saw the magic fade and a future ahead that wasn't for me. Surely not for me? I hid the boy and watched Pinocchio over and over and I wanted to be good and right, bu I knew the world would never let me be that real boy. Born to walk a path that made me hate myself.

I looked back on the past sat in that cell. That first night. I looked around. I was told this was my room. My home. Where I lived. But had already lived a lifetime in a closed cell. I knew that night I wa going to break free from the sentence I had given myself all those year ago.

The steps to change are steep. I had to learn to survive in my new environment. Learn to not be a victim or an offender. I spoke with confidence not aggression.

I learned what toxic masculinity was and how I had been surrounded by it in every male role model I had in my life. I learned what coercive control was and how it had affected my life.

I found hope in the LGBT groups I went to, seeing that each journey is never the same. To find your truth. I saw faces who are still inside now trying each day to be the person no one sees.

I found education and it opened my mind and eyes to a world I never saw. On leaving prison, I continued the educational journey I had started in prison: doing a talk for Dr Phil Heron in Durham University, and later co coordinating a workshop with 'Think like a Scientist' programme at the Prison Learning Alliance 2019 Awards at the Open University campus in Milton Keynes. Since then I have done many talks on being transgender in prison and on education in prison. I have worked with Leeds university and Durham university talking about Criminal justice. I have written articles on loss and grief in prison and being transgender in Sister Magazine and the prison paper Inside Time as well as Pink News. I have read poetry on chapel FM and spoken on BBC London about education in prison, and on prison radio on the work that Prison Education Trust is doing and my own journey, as well an article in the Metro.

I now run my own performance company called StandFast Productions and our first play was *High Risk*. I continue to work with the Inside/Outside course in Durham University and work with the Prison Education Trust and LJ Flanders 'incell workout' pen pal mentoring scheme. My first solo poetry collection, *The Boy Behind the Wall,* will be published by Reconnecting Rainbows in 2021.

I write poetry to tell everyone that whatever labels we have:.. baby, daughter, son, prisoner, ex-offender… we can find our truth. We have the power to say No. We can evolve. We are not just our worst mistake, but both the best and the worst of humanity - if only given a chance.

Overgrown Beginners
Kestral Gaian

You're stood right in front of me,
I wish the ground would swallow you right up,
You tried to be a carbon copy of someone less fortunate,
You suck.

You think you know me, think you understand me?
You're wrong.
Can you even hear me? Up there on your pedestal,
can you hear my song?

Because every other singer,
is an overgrown beginner,
We're drowned out by the rich kids and their ways.
Their shitty little anthems,
About holding Mum and Dad to ransom,
Drown out the words that I want to say.

This isn't a love song,
Mostly 'cause I hate you.
This is a formal address.

You drive me crazy,
Not because I like you,
Although that you had probably guessed.

You pay for all your followers,
and the fakers that all swallow,
every privileged damn word that you say.

You probably had morals,
but found fame in starting quarrels,
with a make-believe fanbase that you've paid.

I am not a wealthy man.
I am not even a man.

But if the complexities of making art
without your father's visa card,
is a concept you find hard,

Then I don't think the subtleties
Of different gender identities,
are really within your grasp.

Stop stifling the poor,
Pick your guitar case off the floor,
Set a more worthy precedent,
And run on home to your country residence.

Because every other singer,
is an overgrown beginner,
We're drowned out by the rich kids and their peers.

Their shitty little anthems,
About holding Mum and Dad to ransom,
Drown out important words that we all need to hear.

Kisses to the moon
Kim

When I'm feeling down
Or when I'm feeling blue
I look up at the moon
And send a kiss for you

When you're feeling down
Or when you're feeling blue
Look up at the moon
And there are kisses there for you

I'll send them up at night
And tell you where they are
And when we both look at the moon
We'll know we're not that far

I'll love you now forever
And I'll be with you soon
But just for now, until I'm there
I'll send kisses to the moon.

Wrong body

Leighton Foster

[Trigger warning: dysphoria, self-harm, attempted suicide]

Do u know how it feels to be trapped in the wrong body?
See in my head it's clear but in yours it's all foggy.
People say I'm being silly when I cry,
but trust me if you were me to the world you would want to say bye.
I've self-harmed over it,
even tried to commit suicide,
but god made me this way for a reason,
so for now I must abide.
I can cry all I want it won't change a thing.
 I just need to accept it's how things are for now
and grow a thick skin.
One day I will be a boy,
my life will be such a joy.
So for now I just need to wait for the time to come,
realise that it's also hard for my mum.
Because yeah I look like a boy but she can still see Lauren,
when I take testosterone Lauren will become less common.
But she needs to realise I am still me,
 because even as Lauren,
 deep down I was really Leighton.
I'll just look different and sound a different way,
 but it's still me,
 me and I'll still be the same.
So I need to accept that my change won't happen yet.
mum needs to realise it's gonna happen,
but Lauren we don't need to forget.
So for now I'll just keep dressing like a boy
and knowing in my head I'm male,
 then one day I'll actually be a man without fail.
So no more tears or trying to commit suicide,
 I'll just wait for the day to come and be who I am with pride.

The Sundae
Beth Mackenzie

I'm home, you're home
Feed me some expensive treats
Please throw me a bone
Wait, the government changed the rules,
there seems to be no way to cheat!

Now we're indoors, there is so much we can do
Remember the unofficial march, and how we planned a trans coup!
"I know, I have some yeast, some flour, some banana instead
My partner of 16 years, I'll bake that bread.."

Afternoon tea, some clapping, the same topic on the radio –
endless news
The government tells me I can't leave our home,
so I'll surf for some cat mews!
Tomorrow will be the another day
Yawn, I'm going to bed early,
yumm to dream of a chocolate flavour ice cream sundae!

Not Dead Yet (lyrics)
The Bleeding Obvious

It's something kooky when people think you've died
And mourn your life before.
The strangest feeling to live in the past tense
And not be called no more.

I'm not a zombie or a spectre of regret
Cos baby I'm not dead yet!
Not six feet under, the grave remains un-let
Cos baby I'm not dead yet!

I'm still walking and talking, get blanked every day
I think I'm pretty strong
"We're always here for you!" the mantra from my friends,
Invisible and gone.

Don't write me off babe, the funeral's not been set
Cos baby I'm not dead yet!
I stand alive and well, as good as you will get
Cos baby, I'm not dead yet!

Lyrics from the debut album *The Bleeding Obvious,* reproduced with the
permission of the artist. https://bleedingobvious.uk/debut/lyrics

Survive to Fight

Paula Adrianne

This girl hates injustice
She stands for what is right
This girl has anger
And she's not afraid to fight

But now she's on lock down
'Stay home' she was told
So now she's had to pause
She's put the fight on hold

She follows all the guidelines
She needs to stay alive
She can only fight the Terfs
If she manages to survive

They thought the fight was over
But they were very wrong
The Terfs are fucking evil
So this girl's fight goes on!

(Written during the 2020 COVID-19 lockdown)

The Discovery of Witches
Sydney Cardew

Scent of beeswax and coffee
Caramel and old leather
Gleaming salve on pale thigh
Thin-haired, and sallow
The belladonna, the aconite
Micronised and esterised
The path to hidden sabbaths in the heart

The outer dancers:
Hazy faces, just behind the eyes
Locked beyond the circling of the years
Screaming in the silent theatre
The burned, the drowned, the walled away
Pricked and pilloried, panicked and pinioned
Cruel flotsam of a careless world
Though nameless, they are honoured guests

Further in:
More concrete forms, all knees and bruises
Their shuddering dance
The ice bath, the electric shock
They hold each other close:
On every side the trees are writhing
The deaths-head flames are licking at their feet
The fascist drums are knocking on their hearts

And the scouts who laid paths for us,
Furtive, stealthy, silent
Their parts tight bound
Their traitorous lips well trained
They form the final ring
They spiral tight around us

Moonlight dances
It catches on our piercings, and our scars
Our hair and nails shimmer, oily rainbows
Our skyclad bodies, self-created art
Our wise familiars hissing at our feet
We lock our broomsticks in a seven pointed star
And strain to turn the axis of the Earth

What if Pride was silent?
Quenby Harley

What if one year we decided to march without the crescendo?
Because we're no longer 50 people, screaming to be heard
A march 40,000 queers strong demands attention
And in a world growing ever louder, sometimes silence hits hardest

What if we said no to the loud, camp party?
Commodified, commercialised, packaged up and used to advertise
If we made this a space for the whole community to share
Welcoming the introverts and neurodiverse
otherwise pushed to the side

What if Pride was about us coming together?
Without the need to perform or conform to the expectations of others
Because we don't owe entertainment to anyone
But within our community, we bring solidarity to everyone

Strip away the cheers and shouts
Take the music and dancers
What's left beneath the glitter and glamour?
A show of strength

And without distraction and diversion
We could look beyond celebration
See the battles yet to fight
Not just those already won

A time to come together
To feel our power
Reflect on our struggle
And remember our fallen

How might that change things?
If it was truly a protest, not a party
A time to think, not to shout
So, what if Pride was silent?

Hang On In There (2020 Remix)
Ash Brockwell

[Trigger warning: anti-trans violence]

So somebody hates you, and everything's dark?
Ignore them. Keep living. The world needs your spark.
There's plenty of haters: sure, that much is clear,
But the thing that annoys them is seeing us here,
So don't check out now, please. Stay here. Don't give in.
Let's keep on annoying them. Don't let them win.

They took out their anger and sadness on you:
We see how it's hurt you, and we're hurting, too:
They've ripped us to shreds and they've ruined our days,
And we're stuck back together in very strange ways.
There's no way to go back and undo the harm,
But our crazy new shapes have… their own kind of charm.

The journey is long but you've travelled so far,
Fought so many fears to become who you are:
And yes, you're amazing! You'll say it's not true,
But there's someone out there who's inspired by you.
There's someone who sees you and loves what they see,
And thinks, 'Hey, one day maybe that will be me!'

It's OK to admit that you don't feel OK,
It's OK not to wash all the dishes today,
It's OK to sigh deeply and go back to bed
When you can't get away from the thoughts in your head;
But what isn't OK is to quit on us now:
Resolve to keep going, and soon you'll learn how.

The kids of the future will look back, bemused
At the way human beings were once so abused
For being themselves and for living their lives;
They'll admire the way that the spirit survives.
So come on. We've got this. The haters can't win.
Keep hanging on in there. Don't ever give in!

la petite mort
RKP

Fink I've bitten my tongue so much,
It's so easy to swallow,
N'hold that breath,
One day I won't - reminds me of...
But blue might be a good colour for me.
Allow, roll'n'tap...
Pass me a lighter for a glowing,
Mind of glass'n'heart of concreate,
Calmly crumblin',
Lost wivvout home to call my own,
Reversing to sand'n'stone,
Cos Asphalt ain't forever.
Take it on the chin fromma,
Skull filled wiv verbal berating.
Inner intuition's gone AWOL,
Equal to physical,
The pain... You've heard it all before, daily.
Heavy beats of fear bang this chest,
L on my forehead and a
Inner cochlear witha mouth fulla red,
Gurgle'n'spit down the drain,
All those aspirations'n'Aries standard,
Crossed out like a trending cancellation,
Diagnose the dose for contamination,
Evidences ain't passed no sell by date,
Infectious and viral,
High level up to the eyeball

Need to learn with it, though,
Want to live without it, still...
So grin and bare broken teef with a bruise the size of a soul,
I'd try and find rest,
But the fears bite me up - bed bugs.
There's always been a parasite in my room.
Insomnia only blinks 40 winks,
When the mytazapine hits.
So sleep tight in capsuled slumbers.
Zero R.E.M,
For the rut I'm in...
Then it's mornin'.
Rinse and repeat to see the effects,
Like wax on wax off from burnin' the candle from both ends,
But before, scratch my back'n'see how bright the matchstick gets,
I'll side burn, rabbit eared, and canoe...
For shits creek and ankle deep.
Swallow baked heat,
Hot rocks for your esophagus
Slow smokey burials,

One for the right,
One for the left,

Fill'em up like that 10% capability.
So many seasons,
But a perfect year ain't one..
Like perennial weeds,
Annual defiance - Horticultural battlefields.
Be careful when pickin'em.
Stem anger at the root of the problem,
Class for Coping mechanisms 101,
Pick noses knuckle'n'down,
Examine'em like tea leaves.
N'lemme know if you've got a better solution.

Rented rooms

Dalton Harrison

[Trigger warning: prison, drug use]

They say this room with its white walls and new carpet
I now rent once housed a smack head
The guy upstairs knew this to be true
Who now spits at me drunkenly
He knows this as fact as they had the same social worker
I think back to that time
I was still in prison
The smack head was still alive
Maybe the guy upstairs mouth didn't smell quite like rotting flesh
My mum was still laughing
Just living in bliss not realising that the cancer was waiting
Like I was waiting to get out
Like he was waiting to not wake up
Like that guy upstairs room mate had not yet been knifed waited for
that bus to take him there
For me to sit not knowing all these things to exist
now makes me grateful I'm alive
Makes me wonder how I made it this far

Tom why are you dressed that way

Red Fraggle / Beck Alsford

[Trigger warning: genitals]

Tom why are you dressed that way
your mates will take the piss
but dad I just feel like a girl
was I just born like this

Gemma stop this football stuff
it's meant to be for boys
but daddy I was born to play
why are you so annoyed

I'm pregnant so I will tell the world
the thing they wanna ask
is what will be between its legs
well this will be a task

Hey why is it your business
if it's an outy or an inny
or whether it is gonna have
a willy or a minnie

Just to keep you guessing
I'll dress them all in white
and keep their genitalia
completely out of sight.

Why A Rainbow
Quenby Harley

Why a rainbow.
What makes it ours?
What do the colours represent?
The flag is an imperfect representation

A rainbow is not discrete
Not 6 distinct colours
But an infinite spectrum
From one edge to the other

Within that there is endless space
Room for nuance
A place for each of us to find ourselves
Labels and boundaries blur as one colour blends into the next

And what we see is only the start
Beyond the visible there's so much more
Incomprehensible to untrained eyes
The rainbow stretches beyond those bounds

Not 6 colours
But infinite shades
Visible and invisible
And within it there's space for every one of us

Don't touch my hair
Frogb0i

[Trigger warning: racism]

I am not 'exotic'
I am not 'half cast'
I am not a 'chocolate man'
I am not 'the shade you want to go'
I am not a 'caramel latte'
I am not your 'token black friend'
I am not a 'US murder statistic waiting to happen'
My colour is irrelevant
My hair is irrelevant
My soil coloured eyes are irrelevant
My genetic background is irrelevant
Don't touch my hair

Blue Flames
Alex Clare-Young

I used to listen when they said,
"Sit down!", "Be polite!"
"Don't raise your voice!"
"You shouldn't be so political."
"Stop arguing back…"

Then I transitioned, I became despised,
And they called me names and spat at me and attacked me,
Stole my innocence and my body. And still, I was polite!
I didn't raise my voice. I wasn't too political.
I didn't fight back…
And my silence burned in my throat like an angel's coal.

Then I learnt,
I listened to other trans voices, year after year,
And I realised that it was even worse if you were
Black or Latinx or Femme or Poor.
And year by year I was less polite,
I started speaking out, I became political, I stood up.
I can still taste the blessing of that burning coal.

Then, 2020, I watched, I listened, lockdown started,
And I realised that politicians control,
The lives of the workers and those who are disabled, and…
People. Are. Dying.
So I stopped being polite for the sake of it,
I stopped falling silent when criticised,
I became a lot less moderate, I started to learn about politics,
I refused to sit down.
I can still taste the blessing of that burning coal.

And then… then…
They said, "Maybe you should use the 'women's toilets'"
…Because I
Sit down!
To pee.
They said, "Maybe you should let people say what they want
About you"
…Because the most important thing is to
Be Polite!
They said, "But we're dealing with a pandemic right now"
…Because they really wanted to say
Don't raise your voice!
and
You shouldn't be political
at a time like this so just
Stop arguing back.

I rose up, I swallowed the coal, I opened my mouth
And blue flames spiralled out, refining my truth:

I won't sit down while young people die.
I won't be polite when you ask it I have a clit or a dick.
I will raise my voice until you see me as I am.
I will be political until the powerful loosen their grip
I will argue back until everyone can speak truth to power.

And *until justice rains down in tongues of fire*
I will spit blue flames at your lies.

My Life - Rev. Alex Clare-Young, UK (they/them)

Some of this story is adapted from my serialised life story blogs at www.transgenderchristianhuman.com. If you would like to read more about me and the things that I care about, or to get in touch, please visit my site.

[Trigger warning: sexual abuse, self-harm, spiritual abuse]

Little me was pretty sure that I was an alien. It sounds funny, looking back. Could I have really thought I was an alien? It is the only way I can describe how I felt as a child, though. Despite privilege and love I felt like an alien. I just didn't fit.

I thought that one day the spaceship would come down to take me home. I longed for that day. Scary, and heart-breaking, when you think about it…

At thirteen my love of music and need for a faster pace of change took me to a different school and – WHAM! – I suddenly knew who I was. Teenage me, 'Yes, of course, I'm a boy!'. I couldn't be, though. 'Girls aren't boys… Are they?', I thought, more alone, more hidden, than ever.

Alienation and hiddenness take chunks out of us. I couldn't sleep or eat, I cut, I lost friends, I gained (bad, dangerous) new friends. I was chucked out of church. I couldn't live at home for a bit. I was so anxious I would throw up. I was abused by a boy. I. Fell. Apart.

I didn't realise back then that people who felt alienated had a special superpower – transformation.

In uni I found mirroring partners, people like me, a church that welcomed me and a youth group where, suddenly, I met trans people. I didn't know that they – we – existed until then. Revelation, joy, excitement. I was 18. I finally knew how I might be able to put the pieces back together again, how to be Alex. Trans. Christian. Human.

At first it was all very closed, I was going to 'be a man', whatever that might mean. I was going to be the manliest man I could be. Basically, I was a total dick.

Thankfully, Spirit breaks open our expectations. The God that is in and around us and woven throughout creation reshapes and recreates us every day and, to me, that recreation is the most loving and grace-filled relationship that we can experience.

I feel that I am caught in a web or a matrix of creativity and growth; and I love it. I can access the whole of who I am, and the most important part of that identity is two-fold; my relationship with God and my relationships with others.

We are not abandoned. We are not alone. Rather, we are created to live with and for others. Being open to the fullness of myself has enabled me to enter fuller and more reciprocal relationships with God and others.

And that grace-abounding capacity for growth and change is what led, and leads, me deeper into and out of myself and those around me. I am a non-binary demi-guy and I allow my identity to be shaped and reshaped daily. I care more about other people than myself and I want to do my bit help change the world. That's why I'm a minister, not despite of but partly because of the oppressive nightmare that is institutional religion.

Together, I genuinely believe that we can enable change, transformation. May it be so.

While We're Here (lyrics)

Ash Brockwell

I wonder what you might attempt,
if you knew you could not fail…
Where would you go, what would you do,
if you were not afraid?
What would you dream, what would you try?
Where would you climb, how far, how high?
Where would you go, what would you do,
if you were not afraid?

Where would you sing, how would you dance,
if you knew no-one would judge you?
Where would you go, what would you do,
if you could break through fear?
What long-kept secret would you share?
What would you give to show you care?
Where would you go, what would you do,
if you could break through fear?

When will we take that leap of faith? We've waited long enough!
When will we understand that we are more than strong enough?
When will we hear that inner voice that waits to guide us,
To light the flame of love that burns so deep inside us?
When will we let determination cast out fear?
When will we realise, when will we realise,
We've got to live each moment while we're here?

What are the words that you would say,
if you could not be rejected?
Where would you go, what would you do,
with a courageous heart?
What grievance would you rise above?
To whom would you declare your love?
Where would you go, what would you do,
with a courageous heart?

When will we take that leap of faith? We've waited long enough...

The songs of those who leave us
often have a common chorus,
Regretting not the things they've done,
but what they didn't do:
The paths not taken, chances missed,
The people that they never kissed…
Where can we go, what can we do,
although we're still afraid?

Today we take that leap of faith! We've waited long enough...
Today we understand that we are more than strong enough!
Let's listen to that inner voice that waits to guide us,
To light the flame of love that burns so deep inside us:
Today we let determination cast out fear;
Today we realise, today we realise,
We've got to live each moment while we're here!

Splendid! (lyrics)
The Bleeding Obvious

Here we are, a job well done
Live for now, what's done is gone
Roof is mended, grass is cut,
Time for a cuppa - splendid!.
This is nice, the shoes still fit,
Could afford that outfit if I wanted it.
The sun's still shining even though it's cold,
Could be worse but it's splendid!

A silver lining's hidden in the clouds
Have faith, what goes around, comes around.

Call your friends, tell 'em the news
The world's OK with nothing left to lose
Lying in the gutter, looking at the stars
Picking it up - splendid!
Life is good, life is great
Have a drink or two with mates
Raise a glass to the friends we've got
Today it's all - splendid!.

A silver lining's hidden in the clouds
Have faith, what goes around, comes around.

G&T - splendid!
Dancing in the kitchen - splendid!
Yellow car - splendid!
Northern star - splendid!
A laugh with your mates - splendid!
Tricky first date - splendid!

Yorkshire Tea - splendid!
You and me...?

Swimming upwards, bit by bit
I can haz burger but I ated it
Someone out there loves you lots
Keep on truckin' - splendid!
Walk the line, walk it good
Don't get caught up in the mud
Throw some shapes and walk through town
Ain't it all just splendid!

A silver lining's hidden in the clouds
Have faith, what goes around, comes around.

Lyrics from the debut album *The Bleeding Obvious,* reproduced with the permission of the artist. https://bleedingobvious.uk/debut/lyrics

Nothing in Particular
Jon/Joan Knight

Listen, hear the silence around the thundering traffic;
Holding planes in air and the cheep of the sparrow.
See past the stars to the infinite black
and feel through warm skin to our aching hollow.
In your touch there are a billion distances
charging apart by mundane forces,
I sense the tingling absence of each one.
Turn to see the colour beneath the rainbow,
look and grasp where it has gone.
In laughter and music, the gracious rests for breath;
In the tumultuous applause of life, the soundless relief of death.
Hear the relationships silent kisses
Be touched by the pressure less love of life
Feel cut to the core by an atom less sliver
on forgiving fringes of strife.
Sense the faster beating of a proud mother's heart,
the dreams of an irreverent child.
Rise now, through the ignorant bawling,
be in silence reconciled.
Far in the empty seams of the universe,
where holes are stitched together,
the nonsensical binding ties lie, singing silently,
the heart of matter.

Pink Wafers
Beth Mackenzie

My partner and I
Spent so much time together, we don't argue, fuss or fight, we fry
Delicious food, vegetarian goodness
Our kitchen, sometimes it's a such a mess!

After 16 years we've heard it all!
"Living in each other's pockets"
"How do you keep it fresh? You could both be heading for a fall!"
We say in retort, we'd never pull out the plug socket!

A pair of old tarts, sticking to it through thick and thin
Like the memories from our colourful biscuit tin
Now we're working really hard in these tough unprecedented times
To make sure we stay strong, and end up
not looking like a pair of limes!

A Quiet (Lyrics)
Kimmy Katarja

(Vs 1)

There's this quiet in me.
 A cool breeze that came
and will never leave,
who cares how loud I sing.
A big white room
and no one listening.
Just a quiet in me,
no matter the dream
no matter what scheme
just a-

I can scream all I want
listen to the loudest of song
but there's still a quiet,
just the quiet.

Corridors of men,
tower tops, and tree friends.
Banging guns and scattered thoughts
in my head.
But the tears can't come from me,
just my friends.
I can't move,
I just wait for time's end.

There's this quiet
Just the silence
There's a quiet
A quiet in me

So I think this is the end,
quiet could me my new friend,
if I fill the void
could I begin to become
it an never be again

There's this quiet
Just the silence
There's a quiet
A quiet in me

I'm not the quiet
I'm not the silence
No I'm not quiet
There's just a-

Messages
Claire Fox

As we dance
as the ripples
reach the shore.

Let's stop.
Let's remember.
What throwing pebbles is for.

Let's remember.
If we stop.
There'll be ripples no more

* * *

I have a message
A message from God
To the church
You're wrong
You're fighting the wrong battles
And if you want to know
Which battles
You should be fighting
Then look at the battles
The outsiders are fighting.

* * *

Our fears
In all their guises
Can steal the music for our dances
But God's love in all its fullness
Creates a duet for all our senses

Life's Plan

Keelin McCoy

This was life's plan for me
I'll be what I need to be
The path was hard to start
But I now have fire in my heart
This journey has empowered my soul
Finally I'm on the way to being whole

Although some turned their backs on me
I've been blessed to meet a new family
Peers that feel my pain
Walk beside me and help me up again
Through trouble and strife
I'm finally happy with my life

I felt I was stuck in a cave
Then my new family helped me to be brave
I wouldn't have it any other way
The new me is here to stay
It took me a long time to see
But I'm at peace and finally ME

Discomfort
Barbie Midna Pyka

I see it everywhere
Male
Female
And you have to pick *one*
But I'm *not*.
I pick female.
Because that's what's *expected*
From someone with a female body
One day though
I won't have to deal with it
That discomfort.
The discomfort of picking
a gender I'm *not*
Someday
I'll snap
Let the world know
I am not *female* or *male*
I'm just *Andy*
Like it or *not*.

There are days where I feel more feminine.
And days where I feel more masculine.
Some days I feel like neither
Or maybe both.
Either way,
I'm still me. I'm still Andy.
Whether I'm they, or she, or he
Either way, I don't deserve to feel the discomfort of picking one.
Because I'm *not*.

My Secret
Aidan Sarson

I have a secret, well most people don't know,
I don't have to tell you, I don't think it shows,
I know that having this option is a very big honour,
I know others aren't able to, even though they wanna.

You look at me now and call me Sir,
No doubt influenced by my facial hair,
But 7 years ago you would have called me Miss,
No doubt influenced by my massive tits.

Blue or Pink
Rebecca

Moments as these, fall loose like leaves,
Drowning in poisonous water.
Man meets Woman beneath the murk,
Father and Son, Mother and Daughter.

Pick a hue from this single pair,
Don't forget to feel a fool.
Wax and wane with winds of life,
Things they don't teach us in school.

Here's your cage, now here is its key,
You be sure to lock up thoroughly.
Plenty will hate, plenty may see,
So clutch it tight and then loudly decree:

I am my own volition, autonomous and free.

Say it Again
Jay Rose Ana

Say it again, say it all again, if you want, then shout,
Really make sure you miss nothing out.
I want to hear it all, shout it loud, every variation,
Hold nothing back, more than words, gimme the whole sensation!

Come on, give it to me, is that all you got?
I'm still here, I'm still standing, is that your lot?
Dig deeper fool, I can take all your rot,
I've taken it before, I'll take it again, come on big shot!

I want you to feel, how it really feels to be you,
And to hate, such hate, come on, you've got it in you!
Let it all out, I'm standing right here, let's really get raw,
And when you are done, start over, I'm ready for more.

And when you run out, when your well runs dry,
I will sit with you, hold your hand, rest your head whilst you cry.
You are not the first, and you will not be the last,
I'm one with my soul, your hateful words will never get past.

Misgendered (lyrics)

Ash Brockwell

Misgendered, misheard, mistreated,
Misunderstood but not defeated, oh
Oh we don't look the same as you
And we don't dress the way you do
But we are human too…yes, really!

Misgendered and still misfits:
We need to use the loo but we can't risk it
Cause they just want to keep us out
We could end up with a smack in the mouth
It's ours for standing out… yes, really!

Siblings, siblings, can't you see,
The future's owned by you and me:
While we're not marching in the street
They think that they've got us beat
But we trans folk won't accept defeat!

We're making our move, we're making it now,
We're signing a new petition:
We want our voices to be heard!
We want our lives, we want our rights
And our identities respected,
We're not a threat, we've done no harm,
Just want to live our lives in peace now,
And that's all!

Waiting list's three years now
Appointment's been postponed and I'm in tears now, oh…
Fuck waiting for the GIC,
They'll never get around to me!

I'll do this privately…
Here's the link, my GoFundMe,
How much is raised now, what's the total? Let me see:
Oh, there's sixty pounds already, so
That's only seven grand to go…

We're making our move, we're marching again,
We're writing to our MPs too,
We need our voices to be heard!
We're tired of hate and Twitter trolls,
We want our kids to be respected,
We're not a threat to women or girls,
Just want to get on with our lives now,
And that's all!

Siblings, siblings, can't you see,
One day we'll get our GRC,
No changing room will cause distress,
Our lives won't be valued less,
And we won't be libelled by the press…

We're making our move, we're making it now,
We're calling on all our allies,
Together maybe we'll be heard:
We want our lives, we want our rights
And our identities respected,
We're not a threat, we've done no harm,
Just want to live our lives in peace now, and that's all!

(Can be sung to the tune of 'Mis-Shapes' by Pulp)

Bird, You Can Fly (lyrics)

Eyemèr

So the time has come
For your soul to finally belong
Stop the facade
Though the world is not ready for you and I

You're starting your life
From this moment now
Bird you can fly
Bird you can fly
You're breaking out
Out of your shell today

You're starting your life
From this moment now
Bird you can fly
Bird you can fly
You're breaking out
Out of your shell today

Kid, you'll be fine
You're not a girl
You're not a boy
Nor am I!

Trapped
Kyle Warwick

Trapped inside my mind,
Or trapped inside my body?
To know my body is wrong
But to think my mind is too

Fear gripped,
Sadness beheld,
Waiting to be set free,
But knowing real freedom
Will take years to gain,
And even then
Will be an expensive luxury

It's funny how
What you take for granted
Could be another person's luxury.
The hair you shave
Could be someone else's lifeline.

It's a dark world,
Knowing your body is wrong,
But it's a scary world,
Thinking your mind is too.

Euphoria and the Vultures
Sydney Cardew

Imagine for me, if you will, a vast and still plateau
An arid upland, silent as a stone
Grisaille waste of dust and and tumbled rock
Undisturbed, except for feeble winds
That stir the bone dry powder of the years
The greyness unrelieved by yellowed grass
That sags beneath the skeletons of trees
No flowers, insects, beasts or singing birds
The feeble sun, remote in dull lead skies

And through this awesome waste a figure stumbles
Robed and veiled in grey, with bandaged hands
Caked in the dust that trickles in the footprints
Scrubbing clean the record of its passage
Only the black shapes wheeling far above can track it
Patient and efficient, malevolent and expectant
They see the abject figure fall at last
A joyous shriek re-echoes from the hills
And they descend, surround the heap of rags
They watch it breathing still, there is no rush
But high above, the clouds are banking

The first drops fall, like hammers, drumbeat slow
Collecting arid dust in fat black clots
The vultures shriek again, one grabs a tatter
It pulls the veil away
and the sky splits open
Her pale face illuminated
As the rain falls upon lips that had forgotten water

A sudden gust of wind; the joy gone from the carrion cries
They take to awkward flight again, ungainly now, absurd
The thunder roars. The grass is turning green
The flowers are opening, the insects swarming
Streams are bursting through the dead ravines
As she stands, the sodden rags hang thin as silk
Revealing her beauty as they fall away
She steps forward, deep footprints in the sprouting loam

She closes her eyes. The rain softens.
The smell of petrichor invades her
Colour comes to cheeks, her red lips smile
And far away, the vultures screaming.

The Boy
Paula Adrianne

[Trigger warning: genitals]

He's not like other guys,
His legs are smooth and long,
His muscles do not bulge,
But he's emotionally strong.

He's not a macho tough guy,
He doesn't pretend to be,
He doesn't use urinals:
He sits down to pee.

He cannot grow a beard,
He knows because he tried,
He bleeds once a month,
His voice is pretty high.

He's a boy without a penis,
A boy who's chest ain't flat:
He's a boy because he says he is,
And that, my friend, is that!

Life
Kestral Gaian

Life at the window,
Life is a curse,
Life lived in shadows,
Life lived in verse.

Life causing trouble,
Life causing pain,
Life lived in cycles,
Life lived again.

Life touched by anger,
Life touched by rage,
Life lived in terror,
Life a torn page.

Life would be better,
Life would be free,
Life could be wonderful,
Life could just be.

Life of 'if only',
Life of regret,
Life knowing our
Life is not quite there yet.

My Life – Kestral Gaian (she/they)

Defining the Undefinable

How do you define yourself? For me, that's been a question core to my life for as long as I can remember. I sometimes like to imagine an alternate universe in which a cis het version of myself has never had cause to question the way they are defined and I'm almost jealous. Almost. Imagine the stability that one must have if they never have cause to question their own identity, their own *raison d'être*! But no. I am the me of *this* universe, and whatever maelstrom of magnificent mediocracy my life has become is mine to own and enjoy.

I remember the first time I told anyone that I wasn't straight. She was my best friend, we were terrified teenagers at a backwater secondary school in the midlands, and I kept trying to get the words out but couldn't quite say it. She eventually put me out of my misery by blurting "I'm a lesbian" out one day whilst we were sitting in my room watching videos, and I was so annoyed that she'd beaten me to it that I rhapsodised about my own queerness for the next half an hour.

Since then, my life seems to have been defined by a number of key coming out experiences - from the time I told colleagues at my part-time job at Safeway, for one of them to accidentally blurt out "but you don't look gay" over the store intercom, through to a university friend stating "you can't possibly be gay, you're not into pink," right through to telling my best friend of a decade that, in actuality, I didn't think I was a cis gay man - or indeed a man at all.

And there was the issue. Every time I came out, I felt like I wasn't really finding a label that defined me - just a label that society seemed to dictate I use. Those same three words plaguing me every time: *what am I? What am I?*

I am me. In a very literal sense, my entire being is nothing more than the sum of my experiences and choices in life. And yet somehow, I am infinite possibility. I am the poetry of a hundred sleepless nights, the heartbreak of lost love, the warmth of every hot meal I've ever consumed. I am transgender. I am queer. I am unique - there's no other creature in the universe who will ever have the same life as me.

So how do you define yourself? For me, I am an experience. And I can't wait to see what comes next.

Someday (lyrics)
Ash Brockwell

You're 'never enough', you're 'always to blame',
You can't change your looks, your pronouns, your name,
Whatever you say, they still turn away;
you're forced to comply.

And so you grow up, just learning to hide:
You shut yourself down and keep it inside,
You're learning your part and doubting your heart,
believing the lie;

They say that you're broken, or evil, or wrong:
Don't listen! You know who you are. Just stay strong.
They tell you you're sinful, and offer to pray:
Don't listen! Don't listen! You'll live as your true self, someday.

You put on the costumes, cover the scar,
Remember your lines, reject who you are:
You'll never explain the depth of this pain,
don't bother to try!

So as the years pass, you're less and less real,
You just give a shrug when asked how you feel,
And still, all the while, you're faking a smile,
and wanting to die...

They say that you're broken, or evil, or wrong...
Don't listen! You know who you are. Just stay strong.
They tell you you're sinful, and offer to pray:
Don't listen! Don't listen! You'll live as your true self, someday.

So never give up and never give in,
Just trust in your heart and change can begin,
The truth that you see is setting you free,
you cannot deny;

We're here for you now, you're never alone,
You've travelled so far, and look how you've grown:
In finding your voice, you're making a choice
to reach for the sky!

It's not you that's broken, or evil, or wrong:
We're in this together, we've got this, stay strong!
Whatever they tell you, just say that you'll pray
That someday they'll listen,
they'll hear you, they'll see you, someday…

Timeline
Robin Swift

8. I shyly ask the hairdresser:
'How short am I allowed my hair?'
'Just below the ears, or you'll look like a boy'.
Doesn't really seem fair.

10. I don't want to wear that Nordic dress
to Viking day at school.
I don a horned helmet, cape and shield.
Think I look pretty cool.

12. Everybody calls me Frank,
A name I plucked from the air.
"As long as you don't call me Becky
I don't really care".

19. I dispose of my childish nickname.
It's time to grow up, you see.
Try on makeup. Buy some dresses.
I don't hate it. But it's not me.

21. My friend reveals his gender.
I'm inspired. I'm a fan.
I wish I was more like him.
But I know I'm not a man.

23. Chose my character for Comic Con.
A boy. I need to bind.
Try on my order. It just feels right.
It's cosplay - no one will mind.

25. I get married to the man I love.
Our wedding - rainbows galore.
No bridesmaids or groomsmen, only people.
Gender's such a bore.

26. I've finally found the words
To explain just how I feel.
I'm not a man or a woman.
I'm non-binary and I'm real.

Tenacity
Summer Wright

They built the camp beside the water's edge
Above a cycling path, and when I woke
I'd clamber up onto this concrete ledge
And watch the runners, though I never spoke
With them. I doubted anyone would seek
To bridge such clear disparity. Instead,
I wrote in verse the words I was too weak
Or scared to coax to speech beyond my head:
That absolute despair is candor's home.
Within a city like a manmade grove,
In tents convened like flowers in a wreath,
I'd found enough of truth to fill a tome.
Beside train tracks, the flow of cars above,
The Allegheny River underneath.

Fifty years
Chrissie Chevasutt

[Trigger warning: dysphoria]

Fifty years in a prison for something you didn't do,
Fifty years in a prison, just for being you.
The last thirty five in Solitary Confinement for something you did do,
Loving your God, your partner and your children.
Now you're on Day Release,
Like, once a month if you're lucky.
And, all the time you suffer with Dysphoria,
Sometimes it rages like a starving tiger with a broken jaw,
It aches like unrequited love,
Like broken bone and torn flesh.
Love is a powerful thing.
Like, nailed to a cross?
For love?
Or was it just a fairy story?
Only love can satisfy my soul.
An insatiable desire for freedom remains, deep down within.
All written with a smile,
Because now
I am known and accepted as I am.

Letting Go
Siobhan Austin

Accepting change means letting go
Whether it's those boots I should have bought in Barcelona
Which haunt me to this day
Or relationships that I've lost along the way
Or just aren't the same as they used to be
Sometimes I think about things like this;
People I no longer call friends
Experiences that I miss having
I feel that I'm mourning not only the life I had
But the one I could have ended up with
And the sense of grief and loss hits me like a train
But it's not healthy to let that sadness sit in your brain

It helps me to visualise so I picture them
The experiences, the relationships
The thoughts and feelings and the expectations
As chalk drawings on stone being washed away
Some of them are bright and colourful and beautiful
Some of them are ugly and grey
Many are a combination of the two
And really I'm better off with them gone

They weren't the entire piece, just parts of a huge path
Covered in art that wasn't meant to last
And new drawings will be done in the spaces made clean
Some I'll never figure out what they mean
Some of them will be similar to what came before
But none will be the same

Yearning
Autumn Barkley

To be queer again
To be held so tight you've no fear again
To take those arms in yours again
To comfort her mind when
her smile has died from tears again
To be queer again

To be queer again
Wandering hands against warm bodies
To be near again
Against every silence a soft breath without virus
To feel dear again
I love her, and I wish a world for us
I need her here again
against my heart, to have it cheer again

To be queer again

Words to a former self
Steffi Star

My heart a miniscule mechanical mechanism,
powered by the main spring of my unfulfilled potential.
Mylar lungs respire hope and exhale possibility.
Every cell of the person I will become within my palm.
Lethargic cornsnakes full of oxygen slithering to and fro.
A bird's nest of wires wheel above my perfect form.
The incessant beep a constant reminder of my fragility.
Premature expectations against all evidence abound.
Possibility improbably pregnant with the labour of love.

The declaration falls from the nurse's lips
with the leaden weight of expectation.
Plummeting to the floor with the certainty of gravity:

It's. A. Boy.

Each letter a gunshot.
Serenity shattered with significance,
only matched by the silence.

Mere millimetres from my ear
I murmur the comfort of a merciful tongue.
These words ever expanding
like the boundaries of our very universe
Vowels and consonants vibrant planets against a jet-black sky.
Eternity, entirety and epilogue.
Drenched in the emotional enormity,
a tidal wave of elation
 breaks across the shores of my heart.

Expectations and presuppositions smash
against the rock face of my love.

Gender boundaries and norms are dissolved
in the salinity of my acceptance.
A protective tsunami of rage
crashes into the rigid cliffs
of societal expectation.

I. Breathe. These. Words.

Precious baby girl.

I see you.

Deep Questions
Doreen Andrewz

Thinking about the Past and the Future
comparing it with the present ...
Now as a woman I still have deep questions
that my body is asking me
Are we going to never have the parts should be with?
Are we never going to be the lady that can roar
like the lion in my soul?
Are we supposed to spend the rest of our life
behind this masculine mask......?

I know who I am
the kind of woman I am
beyond what the world sees ..
Beyond the colors..shapes..identities..and all that
I still stay the same
Little girl
Working hard to be a strong principled African woman...
With a playful side of course

But at the end
even if am certain of me in the inside
I still look in the mirror
and have first put on "Eye Shadow"
to see myself beyond the shades of ....
hhhhmmm let's not go there..

Sexual Health Clinic Phoned

Red Fraggle / Beck Alsford

[Trigger warning: genitals]

Sexual Health Clinic phoned:
"Hello Beck, what is your identity, what are your pronouns?"
To be asked that question is just so profound!
I spend 30 seconds really confused,
Because I'm just so not used....
To having non-binary, and they / them as boxes to tick.
And then the Doctor asked me quickly,
If I'd recently been intimate,
"With a possessor of a penis,
Or a vagina owner."
I wanted to jump through the phone line and hug her.
Another step forward for the Trans and Non-Binary;
We've still so much to fight for,
But this recognition and understanding
Was making-my-day level of lovely.

Punching my Paradox in the Face
Eden Irving

I don't need to creep into the changing rooms, but I do.
Not so I don't rouse beasts of unbridled banter
and hormonal rage around me, no.
I'm an intruder.
My mask? A slanted jawline and several dozen twiddly strands of hair
south of the neck.
Plus, you know, the obvious genital outliers.
Dart past the racks of rucksacks and coats into the cubicle.
It's rank. It's cramped. It's horrific.
It'll do.

I wanna phase into the brickwork, into my own private quarters.
The bog shall suffice.
Layers of clothing unpeel to reveal the invisible schoolyard wounds.
I view life through a Facebook filter.
It's real but it's warped, edited…wrong.
I pass my days with this broken app,
unable to waft the aerosol out of my vision.
That's why I keep looking down,
eyes planted on the cracks in the pavement.
There's no mirrors in them. No reflections or stinging realities.
Just my feet, carrying on. Keeping up the pace.
Avoiding my Frankenstein Monster complex.
I don't recognise my smile.
Teacher's calling,
boys yelling as they leap into action on the football field.
They can live without me.
I realise this now. Years after those school days of listlessness.
Heart and mind merely making do
with the little apartment they're renting out.

But the past is in the past, locked in a scrapbook.
Sealed recollections I can only handle
when the planets align and my world feels…decent.
Dip back in to remember freeze-frame shots of nostalgia.
Gazing eyes meet my own in the pocket mirror and I pause.
Food for thought? Try a banquet.
One I have to gorge it every time
before I can continue my day in relative comfort.

I am a paradox.

I am true, but this…
my vessel of truth is false.
It's not me.
But it is…

Paradoxical quandaries fuel questioning to come in adulthood.
Fears, fury, ounces of euphoria giving me glimpses, chances,
glances at happiness.
I imagine said happiness.
And I know I will thrive.
I imagine coming out to friends, family, strangers in the street
without a second thought.
And I know I will thrive.
I imagine the validation, the affirmation,
the trust in ones I choose to let know.
I imagine the first steps to take, and the next, and the…
well, the last will never come.
Transitioning with each passing day into a me who can give more,
go farther.
A chemical reaction gone wrong in all the right ways.
And I know I will thrive.

If I were to go back, I'd find a mirror.
Better understanding the fog and filters I'm staring into,
let the water settle around me.

I stare at the paradox that is my birth, my past, my body –
knowing it doesn't have to be me.
And I PUNCH it!
And I tell the dysphoria to fuck off!
And I tell the morons who called me weird and strange and stupid
to get fucked!

And I tell myself that I don't have to accept
stereotypes and styles
as set in stone.
That the dissatisfaction, the confusion,
the feeling of the in-between
has a name.
That I'm allowed to say 'fuck it!'
and be someone I'll enjoy being tomorrow.

And when I know I will thrive, I smile.
For that's all I need to get there.

Sonia
Ruth Mills

You loved me as I truly am:
Your Ruth, your wife, your lovely bride.
You gave me strength to be myself,
To free the woman trapped inside.

But time was short for you, my love;
You soldiered on in so much pain.
My Angel shining up above,
I know one day we'll meet again.

It's hard alone, but I go on;
Inspired by you, I chase my dreams:
Horizons distant to explore,
I want to live life even more.

Your song forever in my heart,
I feel the music come alive:
I dance the words - it's clear to see
How much you'll always mean to me.

Pride in Creation
Alex Clare-Young

The Bible says that,
'In the beginning
God created the heavens
And the earth.'

But we also noticed
God drawing the horizons - with a steady hand
They pulled the ink across that liminal space
Between the heavens and the earth.
A tissue thin line where earth meets heaven
And we may meet God.

Everyone knows that
'God separated the light
From the darkness.'

We also found God smiling
As they swirled darkness into the light,
Creating the dusk.
Later, we heard God laughing
As they sparked light in the darkness;
The most beautiful sunrise
Emerging from its hiding place.

Everyone knows that
'God separated the land
From the seas.'
But when we clamber joyfully through rockpools
Or paddle at the shoreline,
Feeling the wet sands between our toes,

We marvel at the way God mixed
Land and sea together –
At the margins.

Everyone knows that
'God created sea creatures
And winged birds'.

My favourite animal is the penguin.
As I record the story of creation,
Should I put the penguins with the winged birds
Or the sea creatures?
And what about the seahorse?
Does it have a place in
This wonderful tale?

Some people say that
'God created *mankind* in *his* own image
Male and *female he* created them...

So now I am seriously pissed off
And maybe God is too!

They've made God 'he' when it should read 'they'
Because the plural terrifies them.
And neutral...
Well, that just doesn't fit into their hierarchical frame!
They changed 'humankind' into 'mankind'
To uphold the patriarchy and
They split the androgyne into two prematurely because
They were focussed on standing out from
All of the other creation myths.

(Oh, and because they wanted to make sure that
People didn't think it was ok to be trans like me.)

And God says the writers missed bits out
Because…

When God looks at
The horizons and
The sunrises and
The rock-pools and
The penguin and
The seahorse and
People who are androgynous and trans and intersex and
Non-conforming like you and me...
Not only does God say that these are 'good'...
God says that they are
- we are -
Beautiful.

And God is so filled with pride
That they can't hold back the tears.

To see an illustrated version of 'Pride in Creation' visit
https://issuu.com/transgender.christian.human/docs/pride_in_creation_2180d
727fd1f07

Alphabet Soup (lyrics)
Ash Brockwell

LGBTQ-QIN-PDOA2-plus?
Even though the length of it is utterly atrocious,
Nothing else comes closer to incorporating all of us…
LGBTQ-QIN-PDOA2-plus!

Lesbian and Gay: come on, you must have heard of those!
Bisexual, Trans and Queer are famous too now, I suppose,
Then Intersex, Nonbinary… oh, help, what can I do?
I'm Questioning my label now! Quick, add another Q!

Pansexual, Demi, Omni, Ace and Aro (share the A!)
Two-Spirit (if you're not First Nations, that's not yours to say)…
I'm sure we're missing someone out! We can't be finished yet?
Let's 'PLUS' the other fifteen letters of the alphabet!

That's one horrendous acronym, it's messing with my head!
The cishets call us SOGIE, like a slice of soggy bread:
Sexual orientation, gender identity and expression -
that doesn't even scan…
Or could we just agree on 'Rainbow'? That might be a plan!

(Can be sung to the tune of 'Supercalafragilisticexpialidocious')

My Life – Dr Ash Brockwell, UK (he/him)

When I was growing up in the 1980s, I never heard the words 'transgender', 'transmasculine', 'non-binary' or 'genderflux'. I think I was 16 before I even met someone who admitted to being a lesbian! At that time, teachers in UK schools weren't allowed to talk about LGBTQ+ identities: there was a law enacted by Margaret Thatcher, that banned them from promoting 'the acceptability of homosexuality as a pretended family relationship'.

It's a strange position to be in, when you know that something doesn't feel right but you don't have a language to understand it. Why didn't I fit in? Why wasn't I attracted to boys? Why was I so unexcited by fashion, make-up and pop stars? *What was wrong with me?* But I kept my head down and my mouth shut, and eventually found a group of fellow misfits to fit in with.

In my final year at university, I fell in love with my best friend. This was not helpful because (a) she was straight; and (b) I'd already joined a religious group that said a firm 'no' to same-sex relationships. I freaked out and moved away – to another continent.

Life went on. A decade went by. I volunteered as a conference organiser, worked on an international research project, started a charity and a safari company, married my research assistant, had two daughters, watched the business and the marriage implode at the same time, and returned to the UK with my girls (then four and seven) in April 2010.

I'm not sure how I got through it - that period of my life is a blur - but it was probably through denial and focusing on my new job as a researcher. Looking back on those years, it's as though I wasn't really there at all. The only parts that stick in my mind are the moments of realising that I wasn't cis-het and didn't know what to do about it. I was working in one of the queerest cities in the UK but still belonged to the same anti-LGBTQ+ religious group; and after two years I hit crisis point. But thanks to a spiritual counsellor whose business card I picked up in a café, I survived, completed the Artist's Way course, took up painting and poetry and pilgrimages, and started writing a novel.

Anyone who's ever tried writing fiction will know what I mean when I say that the trans man who started out as a minor character soon took over the plot! By locating my own story in a different time and place, I was able to defuse the shock and fear that came from the realisation of being transgender, and eventually to come out to friends and family – initially as non-binary and then as transmasculine.

Fast forward three years and I'm now an associate professor in a new interdisciplinary university, with a PhD and he/him pronouns. I've been on testosterone for 18 months and feel much less dysphoric than I used to. I'm looking forward to launching a new project - Reconnecting Rainbows, an online platform for LGBTQ+ creatives to share ideas and collaborate on projects. I still haven't published that novel, but hopefully it'll happen one day!

Balancing Act
Charlotte Greene

Exciting becomes humdrum
Without the mundane

If we suffered no losses
Could we contemplate gain?

Without knowing bitter
Would we recognise sweet?

Success is a stranger
If we've not met defeat

We like to wear sweatpants
To feel good in high fashion

Without things we're not keen on
We might forget passions

As sad songs of heartbreak
Give meaning to ballads

Don't fear falling over
It helps us stay balanced

Are you feeling better?
Frogb0i

How are you?

Have you had the surgery?

How long have you been on hormones?

Isn't that a bit hardcore?

Why would you do that? *And are you feeling better?*

Top or bottom?

Do you self-inject?

What do your family think?

Was the recovery painful? *And are you feeling better?*

But you looked SO good before...

Why did you choose your name?

Are you still in therapy? *And are you feeling better?*

Send us a dick pic?

How is it going babes?

Trans boys are "so soft"

How do you have sex?

Do you have a boyfriend? No? Girlfriend?

Are you straight now?

Were you trapped in the wrong body? *And are you feeling better?*

Prayer to the Crone
Hannah Bx

When I remember you, my future, my shadow,
who tucks unbidden knowledge into the folds of their face,
my belly swings like Venus is cooking in its own mantle,
continents crashed to one and Saturn shed its rings.

Though you're seconds away next to revolutions in space,
you're only recently visible on my horizon: midcentury me,
hair coloured like shoreline, skin like I finally learned how to swim.

Sometimes silver buzzcut, frayed-lace boots, patched denim,
that's you when my stomach grumbles or I miss the joke:
clang of cutlery, conjuring communal chilli cauldrons,
clatter of strings and gravelly croon filling streets with foregone folk.

Sometimes you come to me sharp, willowy and wizened,
billowing cape of hair and cane carved from local oak;
clad in motorcycle leathers despite my veganism, also
chronic inability to wrap my feet around pedals and spokes.

I try to map out how my contours must shift so you fill
the space this body occupies. Some nights I buckle
under the silent weight of griefs not yet weathered,
that you'll carry in your pocket like rosemary leaves.

I pray for the flash of your teeth and tongue forming 'they',
because my pronouns are uh/hem/air catching in my throat.
I call on your refusal of milky tea or dancing delicately,

and I ask that you grow aloe to soothe our throbbing knees.
I invoke your blunt one-line replies to government letters,
your raised fistful of raspberries, your fires gently stoked.

Now the only life insurance I know is dirt-deep connection,
grown so you won't age alone; blessed are the sinners and stimmers
living on the city hall steps until a double moon shimmers
over the river where I offered nothing but a yell of "God let me live!"

Who are you, product of my insistence?
how will our trail of threads eulogise us?
Queer elder; brazen leader; fallen tree;
washed-up relic of the time before?
Autist who outlived every sepia-leaved report?
Who looked people in the eyebrow and said,
"I belong here."
Who knows? I'm just your younger phantom birthing you
into a world I dream wildly, but can't yet fathom.

This is the trouble with our times:
our elders were taken and we became children
floating in oversized coats. Trying to imagine
our grown selves, neck-deep in ghosts.
Know this: I'll wander miles weighed by soaked clothes,
if you'll show me the path of most resistance.
Walk me through your history aisle.
Show me how we survived the systems.

I wait
Hope Lawrence

I wait

For you
To tell me
If you approve
Of who I am

I wait

For you
To tell me
If you will let me
Pray here

I wait

For you
To tell me
If I can read the Word
To you

I wait

For you
To tell me
If you are sorry
For forcing me out

I wait

For you
To tell me
If you will listen
To my story

I wait

For you
To tell me
If you think my voice
Matters

I wait

For you
To tell me
If you will some day
Empower me

I wait

For you
To tell me
If you will some day
Embrace me

I wait

For you
To tell me
If you will some day

Help me
Hear me
Support me
Welcome me
Include me
See me
Love me

I wait

I wait

I wait

Coming Out
Frogb0i

I think I'm still coming out.
I creep back and forth from the closet,
One step out, two steps in.

Selecting my identity out of a musty imaginative wardrobe.
Holding it up to the mirror like a piece of clothing.
Waiting for my brain and my body to sync.
Waiting for my inner voice to tell me that what I am today, is ok.

That I am not "too much", "too weird", "too different".
Two steps out, three back in.
Hours wasted dissecting myself into palatable chunks for others that
would rather watch me burn than extinguish their perception of how
my body "should be".

Their words singe my skin like flames engulfing me in shame that is
not mine.
It is not mine.

I think I am still coming out.
I creep back and forth from the closet.
One step out.

Forward
Keelin McCoy

She, her, it
I've been called it all
It's sometimes on purpose
To make me feel small

He, him, sir
The music to my ears
Feeling accepted
Makes me drink less beers

I thought I was ok
But I could never see the light
Could I just stay female
For the rest of my life?

It certainly would be easier
To stay as a 'tomboy'
How to decide?
Between easyness or pure joy

I chose to ignore the comments
The belittling and pain
I chose happiness
And I'd choose it again and again

My head is held high
I'm always on cloud nine
My head matches my body
I finally feel it's mine.

I knew what I always wanted
It was my goal so I fought
Through pure determination
And a great network of support

The support is still there
For whenever I need a chat
I'm forever thankful to the trans community
Who have always had each other's back.

I started off as a stranger
Who even I didn't know
But I finally found the light
Forward is the only way to go

Father Ash
L. Cable

Now here you go again
Saying what the fuck is gender?
Now here you go again
Saying you wish your son
Was not a fucking bender;
If my father's love is money
Then I am but a lender.

And here I go again
Saying my father acts like ash
A father-son relationship
Shouldn't just pass
And here we go again
Cutting up my dresses
He sets the booth aflame
Every time he confesses

My father says
Father, what sort of father
Have I become?
Now that I am old
And hate my own son?
The vicar says
Son,
You have become a father.

And here I go again
Breaking off my false nails
From Newcastle to Rochdale
I look for my father
We play hide and seek

But every time he gets further.
Now here you go again saying
What the fuck is gender;
I keep my love to myself.
If my father's love is money
Then I am but a lender;
Have you any sons you wish to sell?
If my father loves god
I am a river in Hell.
I know an old man I wish to sell.

His words a lethal angle on my heart,
Like a family portrait cracked from the start.
Line straight down, splits us in half.
My father tears the veil between love and mercy
And the best parts of me are what he wouldn't see.
He scatters ashes for a son he never had like seeds.
Wish I was stillborn and yet I was still born. He stands still, aflame,
I will be born again, with a new body and new name.

We are dead by nature, like a bush fire,
He looks back on me like a sacred salt spire
I get inspired. I grant my own wishes
I have tasted life without him; it is burnt but delicious.
Burn my forest, I will still grow
When patricide adorns you, it's okay to let go.

I will show you Athena
I will show you a goddess walk from her father ash.

Mental Health Issues
Red Fraggle / Beck Alsford

[Trigger warning: depression]

You should be proactive
and get out of bed
but I can hardly stand
with the amount of shit on my head

Your mental health issues
are all in your mind
But I don't talk out my ass
so my brain's not in my behind

Wait months for an appointment
with CMHT
for them to just tell you
you are not crazy

Why is the mental health place
right near to a bridge
maybe you'll help me
if my brain is porridge

Luckily I'm resilient
and currently strong
so I don't need to hurt myself
to prove you cunts wrong

A butterfly prayer
Samantha Smith

For all our friends
Close and far
Living under the sun
Or in the sky with the stars

Do no wrong and patient be
This life is short for you and me
Find new friends and take a chance
Seeds of love in hearts we plant

Forgive the ones who have done us wrong
The light in them is dim not strong
Take courage in who you are
We are blessed & all made from the same star ★

Metaphoria
Elizabeth Crook

I found a worm poking up from my skin
and when I plucked it out I found that I
was fucked from the beginning,
I always wondered why it sucked to go swimming,
I'm stuck in this innings and trust, I miss giving a shit

fuck thinking, I'm stuffed with misgivings with such a big presence
they thrust a bitch into a pit,
I count the seconds till the sentence is up
and I can take my leave of where all these tough prisoners sit

it's much bigger than this and my shoulders are broad,
newspaper soldiers scalding us raw,
this is the coldest of wars, sinister
wing of the rich is bringing winter with it, acidic as vinegar is

as sick as this villainy is, our summer's on the approach,
the sun hovers the coast and love's shone on our boats,
we must bother to float, we can weather the storm;
with transgender applause, we can get the reform.

Our Candles
Purity K Paige

Let's carry our candles
to the darkness:

hopeless, confused,
broken, insecure, angry,
starving, homeless...

It's only our lit candles
that can give them some hope,
but don't be robbed or lied to.
One lit candle
can provide light to thousands.

We should not misuse our candles
because there is a reason
why we are the ones
with lit candles...

let another very miserable, frustrated, depressed,
confused, lonely, helpless person benefit
from your brightly burning candle.

Our candles shouldn't be attached
to race, to religion, to colour, to privilege...

We just have to reach out to our dying world
using the weapons we already have
and those are
our candles.

Can I Have A Quiet Word Please?

Jay Rose Ana

Can I have a quiet word please?
A phrase that grips my throat tightly,
People really want to know.
Of my gender identity.

Am I trans, or non-binary?
How is my inner strength today?
Are my coping skills holding up?
Then they ask, am I straight or gay?

And what kind of bias do I get?
Have some tips, on how to respond.
And then, my mind drifts far away.
And I wish for a magic wand.

So, let me tell you this for once,
And cut through the curious gloss.
I am a human, my own queen,
So, please, release the Albatross!

I am following my own heart,
And not just my Adams apple.
And trying to be good at that.
That's enough for me to grapple.

Maybe, you could think about this?
As I really am quite sure.
You could point your question elsewhere,
As everyone else seems unsure.

If, as you say, I have a choice,
Then please, feel free, to call me Jay.
Nothing derogatory please,
Just Miss, or Woman, if I may.

And, in return, I will address,
You, how you would prefer me to.
Could we agree, maybe, on that?
And move forwards, a step or two?

Of my gender identity,
As you have kindly called it that.
Do me a favour, if you will,
And pop my choices in a hat.

Make the writing really clear.
On those little bits of paper.
Let me pick one out of a hat.
You may explore them all later.

You asked about my coping skills,
I expect they are not too bad.
But if people are mean to me,
I get upset, and sometimes sad.

I do not really know why,
Maybe, they think I deserve it.
But I think it is when, they look,
Inwardly, they are not so keen.

What kind of bias do I dislike?
Unlike this quiet word, right now?
You mean?

I would rather not make a list.
I think you want to start a row.
To sort one hate, from another?
Could you just accept I exist?

Right now.

It is quite simple, if you try,
Reach out your hand, unclench your fist.
So, if you can, can you do you,
Let me do me, fabulously,
Maybe we could even be friends,
But on you, that maybe depends.

Call me when you decide.

Thanks to this brief exchange of words,
I do believe that I now see.
I am the only one of us,
That is really, truly, free.

Disco 2020

(Lyrics to the tune Disco 2000 by Pulp)

Ash Brockwell

It's seven weeks since I set eyes on my mother,

And even longer since you last saw your brother,

You've shaved your hair off now

(It never suited you…)

Did you dream that when we grew up

We'd go for months and never meet up?

No, I didn't either,

Never even thought of it…

So are you climbing the wall?

Does the house feel much too small?

If I came round to call,

No further than your hall,

Well, would you let me in at all?'

And they all said,

'Let's all meet up in cyberspace now,

Won't it be fun when we all dance on Zoom?

Be there two o'clock in the safety of your room…

I know you're home, there's no excuses,

I know you've been living down there on your own,

Since that damp and lonely Thursday months ago…

What are you doing Sunday, baby?

Do you fancy online yoga, maybe?

Hey, hey, please unmute me, baby…'

Woo woo woo woo woo woo woo…

I was the first in my street to go out

The neighbours said, 'What's that all about?'

Oh, I thought I'd love it but I was a mess:

Too many humans, and it caused me such stress!

To the shop, that was as far as I went

I could have exercised sometimes but it meant…

Oh, it meant nothing to me

Cause I'm such a lazy bum

So are you climbing the wall?

Does your life feel much too small,

If I came round to call,

No further than your hall,

Well, would I get a hug at all?

And they all said,

'Welcome to Disco 2020,

Hugging is history, let's just dance on Zoom,

It's better to stay in the safety of your room:

Pour your own drink and let's get pissed now,

Puke in the sink and clean up on your own,

Cause your cleaner's not allowed in, don't you know?

What are you doing Sunday, baby?

Oops, it's blurring into Monday, maybe,

What the actual fuck, it's Thursday, baby!

Woo woo woo woo woo woo woo,

Woo woo woo woo woo…

Completely Unexpectedly
Jay Rose Ana

Some of the best things in life,

Happen through hard work and determination.

Some of the best things in life,

Happen completely unexpectedly at a service station.

Like driving home, one night, on a long commute.

And suddenly, life makes sense.

And even though it sounds totally crazy,

As you pull into the services.

You have made the first fence.

And you cry, happy tears, uncontrollably.

And you want to dance in the rain.

And when you get home,

The tears are of joy.

And you want to dance all over again.

And you find the courage to talk to someone.

And share the sense you found.

And they listen.

And they hold you.

And they smile as you utter every sound.

And they encourage you to be your best self.

Whatever that may be.

Authentically.

And they stand by your side.

So, you do not have to hide.

And you decide, in your own time.

That realising your true gender is one of those,

"whatever that may be" things.

And for the first time, your heart sings.

And life starts new things.

Some bad, some good, and some in-between.

But all those insecurities that weighed you down,

Begin to fall away, as you trust in who you have always been.

And for the first time, you know who you are.

And you realise, you have never been far.

Like being a passenger in the rear-view mirror,

Of your own life, in your own car.

And you start to feel whole.

And you make happiness your goal.

And people smile at you.

And lift your soul.

And they smile at themselves too.

And people talk to you more.

And reinforce your core.

Because they connect with you.

And you find peace.

More than you ever felt before.

Thank you...
for reading our poems and sharing our journeys.

Thanks to everyone

in our global TransVerse community.

Keep on writing!

Thanks to all the people

who have ever helped us to survive and thrive.

Thanks in advance

to all the trans siblings and allies we haven't met yet.

We may have stood on the edge

and stared into the void; but we're still here.

We might be left with scars,

visible or invisible; but we are survivors.

We are transgender and/or non-binary,

and we march on with pride.

#TransPeopleArePeople

#WeWontBeErased

#PoetryIsPower

#OurStoriesGoOn

In love and solidarity,

Aidan, Alex, Alex, Ash, Autumn, Beth, Barbie, Bingo, Charlotte, Chrissie, Claire, Dalton, dee, Doreen, Eden, Elizabeth, Elliott, Eris the Vogon, Eyemèr, Ezra, Hannah, Hope, Jani, Jay Rose Ana, Joey, Jon/Joan, Kai, Kay, Keelin, Kei, Kestral, Kim, Kimmy, Kyle, L., Leighton, Mattie, Megan, Mickie, Paula, Purity, Queen Victoria, Quenby, Rebecca, Red Fraggle, RKP, Robin, Ruth, Samantha, Siobhan, Steffi, Summer, Sydney, Te Urukeiha and The Bleeding Obvious

List of Contributors

Aidan Sarson (he/him): I'm a trans man, middle aged, no you'd never guess if you met me! I came out to a few aged 27, went back in at 29, tried to live a 'normal' life, it didn't go very well, then aged 39 I came out again, finally got to the point where I thought, `I can't live like this anymore'… five years on and I've never been so well balanced before! Poetry happens when inspiration strikes, sometimes it's bad, sometimes it's good!

Alex Clare-Young (they/them): I'm a transmasculine demi-guy in my late 20s, and I offer support and advocacy for trans people and education for churches, schools, and workplaces. I came out as trans in 2010 whilst studying music in Manchester, worked in a university chaplaincy for two years, and trained for ministry in the United Reformed Church. I started ministry in August 2019 and now run an online church called Churspacious alongside doing research for a PhD re the theologies of trans* people. I live on the Yorkshire Coast with Jo and Digger and we love walking on the beach and swimming in the sea. I have also written a book about my journey so far; *Transgender. Christian. Human.*

Alex Francis (he/him): Transitioned 18 years ago. Tormented, confused, bemused, caring, scared, lamenting, microcosmic, melancholy, frustrated, wondering. Hate ignorance and those evil psychos that torture others, bigotry, cruelty to animals, hangovers, celebrities, violence. Love music, creating, art, sleeping, stargazing in the park, smiles, cats, dogs, seafood pizza.

Ash Brockwell (he/him): I'm a trans artivist (that's not a typo), a project consultant, and an associate professor in interdisciplinary studies. Life really did begin at 40 when I started my transition. I initially came out as genderfluid, then as a trans man, and eventually settled on 'non-binary transmasculine flux' - but that's a bit of a mouthful, so 'trans guy' will do. I love rambling (in both the walking and the talking sense!), painting, cooking, creating rituals and learning Amharic, as well as writing novels, poems and song lyrics. I live in the south of England with my two teenage daughters.

Autumn Barkley (she/her): I'm an anarchist-syndicalist transgender woman and privacy nerd. I wrote my first piece after 2 years of negligence by the British state in reforming the Gender Recognition Act, and my second from queer yearning and nostalgia about partners while in locdown. My third was motivated by my guilt in not living to the ideals I'm about to express, after being given NHS treatment. We must recognise, if these words are to make any difference, that each of us is only free when all of us are. On that, I leave you with a quote: *"We are going to inherit the earth; there is not the slightest doubt about that. The bourgeoisie might blast and ruin its own world before it leaves the stage of history. We carry a new world here, in our hearts. That world is growing in this minute."* - Buenaventura Durruti

Beth Mackenzie (she/her or they/them): Living with my partner for 16 years in the sunny climes of Bournemouth, UK. I love to keep fit and healthy, occasionally can be seen running to the quiet sandy beaches in the mornings. Weekdays I am a software developer, proud of my work as a Civil Servant in Scientific Computing. I work alongside scientists who monitor vector-borne illnesses to improve the health of the UK. At other times I can be living it up listening to disco, deep house or jazz, chatting to my BFF or dreaming up ways of going camping in the Shetlands!

Barbie Midna Pyka (ge/gem, they/them or he/him): Call me Barbie, that's my pen name. I'm twenty years of age. My birthday is in late August and I'm a Virgo. I love bath bombs and I've been writing poetry since I was ten years old in 5th grade. My favourite kind of poetry to write is Spoken Word. I've known that I'm trans for almost four years now. Currently, I use the label genderfluid, though whether or not that shall remain true four more years from now, I'm not sure. The flag sure is nice though.

Bingo Allison (they/them): I am an autistic, transfeminine, genderqueer person, and also an ordained curate in the Church of England. I am married with three small children. As well as moderating a Nonbinary Christians Tumblr blog and posting various poems, prayers, and stories for use by transgender and nonbinary people, I volunteer with the Chesterfield youth group run by Derbyshire LGBT+.

Charlotte Greene (she/her): From the rural English west-country, I describe herself as RTFM. A computer geek since the 1980s, I avoid the modern internet like the plague. I think of my writing as arranging words to paint pictures, weaving intricate patterns with language, intonating tactile textures, embroidered with music and song. With an engineering background I design and builds furniture, recently moving from wooden cabinets to explore softer, upholstered pieces - comfortable, and stylish as well as functional. I love to cook, and took to growing vegetables after losing my father - a keen gardener whose spirit is never far from a vegetable plot.

Chrissie Chevasutt (she/her): Being different as a child was a continual awareness for me. Bullied by boys, at home with girls, I knew I was other. 1976 and Lou Reed's album "Transformer" came out. That was my only education and information I had about my condition. I narrowly escaped prostitution as a transvestite. Drug addiction was my means of dealing with the pain of being 'other'. Opium addiction and begging on the streets in India, I met Jesus for the first time. Missionary, Pastor husband and father followed. Age 55 I had a second breakdown in which I realised I have been transgender all my life. Finally I'm at peace.

Claire Fox (she/her): I am a transgender woman who still spends some of her time presenting as a man. It is often said that I didn't choose to be trans. But if it were a choice, I would make that choice. The word trans means that I am out of the box. It gives me the freedom to explore who I am. It doesn't mean I am not afraid, but it means that I have learned to face that fear. It means that I can have faith in Christ when I am told cannot be a Christian. It is an incredible gift. Thank you, God!

Dalton Harrison (he/him): Transgender male. I have started a company called StandFast that is involved with poetry and theatre performance. love writing. Expressing myself through words. This is home to me. My self-reflection is formed out of poetry and stories. This is how I release my emotions. This is what forms the blueprint of my life. I see life as a journey and it forms my own self narrative. Inside my writing I explore issues such as identity, guilt, loss, incarceration, redemption, society as well as hope and love. But above all that each step forward is a new adventure.

dee b parker (she/her they/them): singer/songwriter - artist/filmmaker - finally transitioning in my fifties after decades of denial despair and defeat feels like a wonderful return to the source code, i knew who i was at a very young age but there were no Mermaids in the 70s, just conversion therapy and 'man up' conversations. Well i tried, but not very well, living (at least) a double life left me only a filtered connection with consensus reality, pouring my energies instead into worlds of my own making. Now with the filters off, i am writing my first book, and recording my first REAL album...

Doreen Andrewz (she/her): I'm a trans woman. I'm 28 years old and I'm from Uganda. I've been a refugee for now four years, in Kenya. I spent some time in Nairobi, and now I'm in Kakuma for the past six months. I'm also a trans rights activist and a human rights defender. I'm the Assistant Executive of Refugee Trans Initiative and I'm also going to mobilise in Kakuma. I try to stand for the rights of transgender people – to stand against injustice that we go through, to see how best we can fit into the community and see how we can live our lives, right through the trauma and struggles of our identity, and how best we can be productive in society.

Eden Irving (they/them or she/her): I am a 21-year-old Creative Writing student and have known I'm non-binary for roughly a year at time of writing. These poems were written at the start of the pandemic; back when I was closeted, for a time quarantined and pretty bloody overwhelmed with life. Since then though, I've come to better experiment and explore who I am among friends and peers, and I owe so much to them for helping me get to the place I'm at now. Even with this hindsight, looking back at the poems I wrote so soon after working out my gender is a surreal experience, and a time capsule of both lockdown and coming out that I'm so glad to have written.

Elizabeth Crook (she/her): I'm a 22-year-old binary trans woman and I live in the south of the UK. I'm pansexual, polyamorous and I have ADHD. I'm also a sex worker. Writing poetry has been an interest of mine since long before I transitioned, and I generally tend to focus on wordplay and rhyme scheme – I originally started out writing rap lyrics, as a die-hard fan of hip-hop. My biggest inspirations are MF DOOM and Earl Sweatshirt, among many others. May my writing bring you the driftwood that your soul may float upon amidst the murky sea that are the times within which we wade. You can find me on Discord! @princess-sock-cat#1234

Elliott Boot (he/him): I'm a 25-year-old trans man from Sheffield. I currently work in children's entertainment but have previously studied a BA degree in Drama and Musical Theatre and a MA degree in Songwriting and Production. I didn't come to terms with being transgender till I was 23. Since then, I have been dedicated to my transition and finally discovered this new found self-confidence and happiness within myself that I never believed I had. Since this, I have been able to pursue music again and have written about how I have overcome my challenges. (See 'Real Life Stories' for more).

Eris the Vogon (she/her): Recently out trans, lifelong eccentric. trans pacifist, too confident in my identity to fight about it.

Eyemèr (they/them): I'm an indie singer-songwriter trying to make your eyes water or at least touch your soul. 'Bird, You Can Fly' is the fifth track from my EP 'Good Mourning to You', which available on Spotify, Apple Music, iTunes, Google Play and Amazon. You can find all the links to my music, videos and social media sites at https://linktr.ee/eyemermusic.

Ezra May (xe/xem/xyr): I grew up in San Diego, first homeless then in foster care. I was always an odd duck. Between moving a lot and social issues I learned later were Autism Spectrum Disorder, I found myself drawn more and more into reading, writing, and other art forms. I worked in healthcare as a Nurse's Assistant in Tennessee until I started my transition, when I moved into retail. My spare time is spent with fantasy or horror shows and movies, queer fanfiction writing, painting, and rock shows. My goal is to be an advocate and give the voiceless their say. My next adventure is in Ohio.

Frogb0i aka Kai Frog (he/they): I am a black trans nonbinary creative, performance artist and queer activist. I'm the founder of "POC Queer Magic" an online support group est. 2018 for queer people of colour. I enjoy making cheese & bean toasties, playing with my cat Muffin and watching queer lgbtqia+ film. More of my work can be found at www.frogb0i.com or @frogb0i on Instagram.

Hannah Bx (they/them): I'm an amorphously non-binary poet living in Southampton and by now a familiar face of the city's spoken word events. Words often elude me in daily life, but they come through in poetry. It helps me find comfort in the liminal spaces of life and my identity. I enjoy writing raw emotion, surreal scenes, and immersive imagery, so my poems become reflections and dreamscapes that play with the fluid chaos of time, nature, and queerness. When I'm not creating, I'm taking part in local activism and daydreaming on long walks by the river.

Hope Lawrence (she/her): I'm a woman who is trans and Christian. I struggled for over forty years to find new ways to cope with dysphoria. As my mental and physical health deteriorated, I finally accepted that transition was essential to my survival. In becoming Hope, I've grown to understand that accepting and embracing my gender identity was not simply about surviving but about becoming whole. Most people rejoiced with me and celebrated as I began to live authentically, but a few did not. They didn't understand the power they held, and how vulnerable I was. It hurt. But I am healing.

Jani E Z Franck (they/them): I am a nonbinary multidisciplinary artist working in visual art, land and site-specific installations, performance, music as well as poetry. I belong in the intertidal zone, the pause between beats, the spans of bridges and the edges of accepted reality. My art plays with symbol and ritual, blending the personal with the universal, exploring the links between ancient knowledge and where humanity is heading in these turbulent times. I embrace the liminal space of existing as bigender/genderfluid and the ability to walk between more than one set of different worlds.

Jay Rose Ana (she/her): I am a civil servant, living with my family, near the centre of Worcester, having moved to the area in 2019. I was recently elected governor of the local language college and, as a transgender woman, I am a supporter of Pride and the LGBT+ charity Out2gether, based in Worcester. See https://www.jayroseana.com/

Joey White (he/him): If you're reading this, thanks for taking some interest in me! My name is Joey, and I'm a trans man that is lucky to have an amazing support network of friends and family. I consider my father to be my best friend, which is a luxury many trans folk don't have. Being a man that is both transgender and fat has meant that I am used to my body being seen or portrayed in a negative light, or even treated as if it were public property. Through words and through comedy I hope to break down these barriers, open minds, and maybe give a few little chuckles along the way.

Jon/Joan Knight (he/him): Born 1975 Jon Knight, I realised I was also Joan from the age of 4 onwards. I suppressed my female being from the age of 11 to 16 due to a homophobic climate at school, I carried on being Joan whenever I could in private. Then a close teacher friend helped me come to terms with who I was and Joan and Jon now share a genderfluid me. My wife and children have been beautifully supportive of us/me! I am a Quaker and a teacher and I truly hope that one day people will be judged solely on how they behave toward one another, not on gender, sexuality or sex.

Kay Whitehurst (she/her): I am Kay, a trans woman from the Midlands (UK). I transitioned in 2018 and am due my second surgery opinion in September 2020. Poetry has always been my go-to medium for relieving my dysphoria and depression and coping with my darkest thoughts and fears. Poetry flows for me, like water from a tap. It is my hope that I can convey to the reader a sense of my being, and so validate my own state of mind.

Keelin McCoy (he/him): I'm 34. I started transitioning in 2012 and only have one operation left which is the erectile device! I live in Wales, UK and I'm a registered close protection officer (bodyguard). Married to a beautiful woman for two years. That's it really!

Kei Patrick (she/they): I'm a musician and poet. I love performing live to music, with space in the middle and silence at the end. People find my workshops 'generous', 'loving', 'safe'. (Tate Britain, Firstsite, Supernormal). I'm intrigued by all things ambiguous. I read lots of philosophy, sci-fi, fantasy… I consider myself non-binary, or trans. want to experiment more with collaboration: writing in a group "illustrating" visual art, writing across languages. Get in touch and we can write together: https://keiwordsblog.wordpress.com/

Kestral Gaian (she/they): I've been asked to write 100 words about myself. I suppose I could, if I put my mind to it, write tens of thousands of words about my life - so where does one begin when having to narrow it down to just a few sentences? I'm a transgender activist, producer and writer with an obsession for baking bread. But what do those things really tell you about me? How do I really distil my years on this plane beyond a few titles and verbs? Well, anyway, enough posturing. I should start writing. How many words do I have left?… Oh.

Kim (they/them): I work within the queer community providing perinatal support for queer families. I'm a multidisciplinary artist who loves to write. I have been writing poetry and prose since my early teens. I also enjoy painting and making jewellery from salvaged objects. You can see more of me at www.thequeerdoula.co.uk.

Kimmy Katarja (they/them or she/her): I'm Kimmy Kat for short, a Black 23 year old Creative born in Jamaica and raised in Cleveland Ohio. Pre-Quarantine I usually spent my days teaching dance and musical theatre techniques to children and by night I take the stage as a drag queen. Podcasting is also how I shake the creative nerve, Under the Wig is the podcast I co-host with my Producer. The songs I wrote, are songs that come from the glittery depths of my heart.

Kyle Warwick (he/him): I am a 20 year old trans man from Swansea. I am into sports, particularly football and rugby and also enjoy writing poetry. My poetry is usually based on personal experiences and feelings and I tend to just write whatever comes to mind. I come out as trans in 2018 and have had a rather eventful life since, however, I am now making the positive changes to my life that I have been needing to make for a long time. My main hopes for my transition are hormones and top surgery but would like to fully transition in the future.

L. Cable (he/she): I am an eighteen-year-old, trans/non-binary poet living and working in Leeds. I am a founding member of the No Larkin About young poetry collective, and host spoken word nights around East Yorkshire. I write about trans feminism, body positivity and love. My debut poetry collection, *Strawberry Fields*, is available now.

Leighton Foster (he/him): I am a transgender male. I have suffered all my life with mental health. I have struggled with addiction and have been inside prison. I use my poetry and singing to vent out my emotions as well as show others who I am. The journey may be long, but the words I have learnt along the way may inspire others.

Mattie Mamode (they/them): I'm a brown queer dyke endlessly screaming into the void. I work primarily in theatrical performance spaces (writing, directing, choreographing) while also writing short fiction and poetry challenging ideas about trans identity, race, disability, religion, and sex work.

Megan Nightingale (fae/faer or she/her): I am a freelance poet, political journalist, disability rights activist and a student. I study Sociology and am based in Liverpool, England. I am honoured to have been asked to write in volumes one and two of trans*(verse) and hope my mediocre poet ramblings can reach and support others! If you like Twitter, feel free to follow my ramblings at @mocc_night

Mickie Leigh: I'm non-binary and have two genders, male and female. Sometimes it feels as though I'm in-between genders. I only realised I was transgender a few years ago.

Paula Adrianne (she/her): I'm a 50-year-old pansexual trans woman, trying to stay safe and sane in a mad world set to self-destruct. I use poetry and activism to fight against bigotry and fascism, and have been rumoured to be the head of the Leeds trans mafia. I do all this whilst struggling with multiple life-threatening illnesses - my mantra is 'Don't dream it, be it'. For more of my work, go to `Paula's Poetry Palace` on Facebook.

Purity K Paige (she/her): I'm a trans woman and a radical human rights activist, and yes I AM black and proud of it. I'm a patron at Refugee Trans Initiative, former Assistant Director of Refugee Flag Kenya, and former Communications Advisor at Refugee Coalition of East Africa. I studied at Makerere University in Uganda and now live in Kenya.

Queen Victoria Ortega (she/her): I'm a proud, brown and plus-size Latina. I believe in leadership through service. I am the CEO of Royalty Consulting Services and work alongside various NGOs to increase their capacity to work with people of Trans experience. I am also the President of FLUX, an organization based in the USA dedicated to creating content that promotes positive images of trans people. I leverage my intersectionality to advise and guide organizations and systems.

Quenby Harley (they/them): I am unapologetically fat, non-binary, and fabulous. A queer writer, performer and activist based in Leeds, my work explores themes of gender, sex (the fun sweaty kind, not the one assigned at birth), and community. My ongoing project *Trans Joy* creates a space to focus on the positive side of trans experience, while my work elsewhere covers a broader range of emotions.

Red Fraggle / Beck Alsford (they/them): I am Fraggle, Lord High Filth Wizard. Morris dancer, Elf Mage, Crafter and Artist. Trans Activist, Leftie, Ink-eater, Introverted creature. It appears someone has given me a platform to spout gibberish, I am therefore more than willing to do so with aplomb.

Refugee Trans Initiative is a non-profit, non-governmental organisation in Kenya that aims to ensure that refugee trans voices are heard and to create freedom and dignity for trans refugees. They have established a safe house for trans refugees who face eviction and mob violence and often fear for their lives. The founders of RTI came to Kenya as refugees from Uganda and the Democratic Republic of the Congo.

RKP (they/them): I'm a gender queer drip artist, photographer and poet who doesn't shy away from exposing heartfelt raw words and nerves. Found at various Open Mics and Poetry events, born in the East and brought up in Cambridge, inspired by life & all things creative; I'm a colourful 'Jack of (almost nearly) all trades' and have been described as 'a pensive wordsmith who daringly invites the audience in to listen to their inspired "destructive yet fun" autobiographical poems'. For more info please see https://www.facebook.com/RKP.Poetry/

Robin Swift (they/them): I am a non-binary artist working in an advertising agency in Southampton. I grew up in Chesterfield and studied animation at Bournemouth University. I have always considered myself a Jack of all trades when it comes to art and I am always open to trying new things - poetry being one of them! I discovered my gender a few years ago and have found so much comfort in the trans and non-binary community, both online and in Southampton.

Ruth Mills (she/her): I am a trans woman and live in Sheffield. I lost my wife to sepsis in October 2017. I work as a software engineer. When I'm not working, I like Roller Derby, riding on steam trains, and composing music.

Samantha Smith (she/her): I'm a trans activist, sexual health volunteer, TDOR [Trans Day of Remembrance] organiser, and a police and equality LGBT panel member. I'm currently volunteering with Citizens' Advice as a witness support outreach worker. I work voluntarily supporting vulnerable and intimidated victims of crime. I'm also an animal rescuer and owner of my beloved posh dog.

Siobhan Austin (they/them): I'm a non-binary person living in Southampton with my husband and three cats. I've lived with mental health struggles my whole life, which have prevented me from doing a lot of things I had once planned for. But they meant I had to learn to use my voice and articulate what I feel. I'm not always good at doing that in conversation, but writing it down seems easier. I feel very strongly about my trans identity and try to advocate for our rights wherever I can.

Steffi Star (they/them or she/her): I'm a gender fucky trans woman who is a bisexual and kinky relationship anarchist. I live with 4 cats, a dog and two terrapins and two lovely humans. I've been writing poetry since I was a wee lass and was first published at age 11.

Summer Wright (she/her): I am a 23-year-old trans woman with a penchant for sonnets who survived chronic homelessness with the help of poetry. I've been published in the Hustling Verse collection, among others, and am now happily housed in Texas.

Sydney Cardew (she/her): I am a young poet and visual artist from the Isle of Wight, a small island off the south coast of England. My poetry deals primarily with themes of nature, transience and my experiences as a transgender woman living in an isolated rural milieu.

Te Urukeiha Tuhua (he/him): I am a trans boy aged 13 who lives in Nelson, New Zealand. I'm autistic and Maori. I'm definitely an introvert. Some things I enjoy are reading and doing ballet. I recently started pointe work. I first started writing poetry when I was 11, because that was when I found out my crush didn't like me back and I felt the need to pour my heart into something. Nowadays I write all sorts. One more thing about me: I love chocolate!! It is amazing and I don't understand those who find it meh.

The Bleeding Obvious (she/her): I'm a one-woman LGBT+ cabaret, currently heading into the realms of disco-funk as a prelude to my third album, Dirty Blonde. The second, Rainbow Heart (from which some of the lyrics included in this book are taken) led to a nationwide tour with dates in Bristol, York, Nottingham, Brighton, Leeds and Manchester, among others. I've played to a busy off-West End theatre for Pride In London and led a thousand-strong crowd in a singalong of *One Girl Girl* at Wakefield Pride. For someone who didn't want to do live shows, that's something of a turnaround! See www.thebleedingobvious.uk

Index of Contributors

About Reconnecting Rainbows

The 'TransVerse' anthologies are published through Reconnecting Rainbows, a platform created by Ash Brockwell (Green Spiral Arts) with Kestral Gaian, Vivi Vix L'Amour, TransVerse contributors and other LGBTQIA+ artists, with a vision of enhancing mental wellbeing through creativity.

We bring people together to publish, perform, exhibit and collaborate across different art forms. Our focus is on work that raises awareness of the issues faced by the LGBTQIA+ community, builds solidarity, boosts confidence and self-esteem, and celebrates gender euphoria and rainbow joy.

At the time of writing, our current and planned projects include:

- *Songs of Remembering: Singing Our Broken World Back Together,* a collection of stories, reflections and lyrics by Ash Brockwell, with a practical and guide and songbook for rebuilding community and restoring our collective sanity

- *The Boy Behind The Wall,* an autobiographical solo collection of poems and stories about life in and out of prison by ex-offender and trans educator Dalton Harrison

- An anthology of poems, song lyrics and life stories by Black trans and non-binary people in Africa and the diaspora, guest edited by Namupa Shivute in Namibia

- An anthology of life stories, meditations, poems, hymns, prayers and liturgies by trans and non-binary people of faith

For up-to-date information about our first published anthology (*TransVerse: We Won't Be Erased!)* and upcoming projects, or if you're an LGBTQ+ writer and would like to submit a collection of poems or look for collaborators on a specific theme, please visit our website:

www.reconnectingrainbows.co.uk.

Getting Support

If you're struggling with your mental health, or experiencing difficult or upsetting thoughts, please reach out – you're not alone. There's help available from trained counsellors whose job is to listen and be supportive.

Here are some helplines and crisis support organisations that we're aware of, at the time of going to press. Please note that this is not an exhaustive list and that contact details may have changed. If your country isn't in the list, please refer to www.ecosia.org or your favourite search engine.

Australia

Lifeline: 13 11 14

ReachOut: https://au.reachout.com/articles/lgbtqi-support-services

Canada

Trans Lifeline: (877) 330-6366

LifeVoice: https://www.lifevoice.ca/crisis-supports/lgbtq-crisis-supports

Kenya

Transgender Education & Advocacy: https://transgender.or.ke/

United Kingdom

Samaritans: 116 123

Switchboard LGBT Helpline: https://switchboard.lgbt/

Mindline Trans+: https://mindlinetrans.org.uk/

LGBT Foundation: https://lgbt.foundation/helpline

United States

Trans Lifeline: 1-877-565-8860

AFSP: https://afsp.org/lgbtq-crisis-and-support-resources

The Trevor Project (youth): https://www.thetrevorproject.org/get-help now/

Lightning Source UK Ltd.
Milton Keynes UK
UKHW020620200123
415672UK00011B/1406